Codecrafter

Erica Sandbothe

To my mother,
who taught me to write.
And to my father,
who taught me mathematics.

Acknowledgements

I would like to thank everyone who had a hand in bringing this book to light.

I would like to thank Heather, who manually debugged my code, and Sharon, who taught Rushingfoam everything he knows. They are codecrafters if ever there were.

I would like to thank my mother and father, for starting me on this road, and Evan, who insisted that there was something special about Tilde all along.

[0]

The power is in the words. These words:

```
% ssh user@tilde.sorcery.codex
```

Anyone with the words may navigate the subdirectories of spells, enchantments, and commands that govern the world. They may examine the codes that allow the plants to grow and thrive, the sun to rise and set, the moon to wax and wane.

Or they may use the words, and write their own codes.

This power is difficult to come by. In the land of Sharell, no human is born knowing how to command water, earth, air, metal, or fire.

Some, however, learn the words.

[1]

The riders were gaining. Tagg risked a quick glance behind her and swallowed, crouching low over her horse's neck. The mare, a sedate, ladylike creature, heaved and panted, her short legs pounding the sandy soil.

"Keep headed west," shouted Shory. Tagg turned just in time to see her bodyguard slow his horse.

"No!" she cried. "Come with me!"

The wind whipped her scarf around her head, but she could still see the mad grin on Shory's face as he drew his sword. Part of her wanted to stop, to turn and stay with the man who had been her protector on the long road from Morthigern. Her father would not run away, not when a friend was in danger. But her father had told her to obey Shory. She whispered an apology and spurred her mare on.

When I am a sorcerer I will not run.   When I am a sorcerer I will not be afraid. A quick look back showed her that Shory had engaged the riders. One had fallen, another was locked in combat with her protector. How many there were in total, she did not know. Shory called them bandits, but bandits would not pursue a target so doggedly. Especially not after Shory had killed six of them already.

Tagg heard hoofbeats out of rhythm with her own. A set of riders had split away from Shory and were galloping straight toward her.

If only her father had taught her *real* sorcery! Then she would have her own staff, and a spell would send the riders flying, their horses' legs tangled in endless knots, their breath swept away from them, their bodies weak and powerless against the might of her codecraft.

The land sloped downward, and Tagg glimpsed the lights of Tilde ahead. Her mare skittered on the sandy gravel, hoofs tangling in the long seagrass that grew on the clifftop flats. Tagg reined her in just in time to avoid sliding down the dune, but the mare's heavy breaths told Tagg that they could gallop no more. She urged the horse into a trot and drew her knife. Her heart pounded in her chest. She would have to be quick.

Hoofbeats. Tagg glanced behind her and saw a rider come into view at the top of the dune. He reined better than Tagg, and his horse danced to a stop. The rider's face was weathered and sharp, and when he saw her foam-flecked horse, he smiled. He drew his sword.

After they had been attacked at Plainfoot, Shory had taught her where to cut a man to cripple him. She slashed as the rider came at her, eliciting a laugh as he ducked out of her range. She hadn't even pierced his leathers.

"Put that down, dearie. She wants you whole, she does, but if you cross me I swear you'll regret it."

It was the last thing he said. Shory was there, his face bloodied and full of anger. He raised his sword and the enemy toppled from his horse.

Tagg shuddered. Shory wiped his sword on the dead man's tunic, then gripped her by the forearms and forced her to look at him. Shory's face was blood-spattered, but his eyes were sane.

"It's over," he said.

Tagg tried to draw herself up in her saddle. It was funny, her governess had never taught her how to thank a man for killing well. Perhaps there was a formal response, and Tagg had simply not been paying attention. Soon she was giggling, and Shory pulled off his cloak and wrapped it around her as the world grew fuzzy and her chest began to hurt.

"We'll camp for the night. Tilde tomorrow."

* * *

It was full dark when Shory woke her. He passed her a bit of warmed cheese on bread, then sat down to stir the fire. It took a while for Tagg to come back to herself. Shory had cleaned away the blood, but she shivered when she remembered the way the man had collapsed.

"The camp's secure, Lordsdaughter. We'll see any bandits long before they see us up here," said Shory, looking out over the sandy flats and low dunes.

Tagg followed his gaze, then huddled back in her cloak. "They're not bandits, are they, Shory?"

Shory looked at her with surprise. "Why would you be thinking that, Lordsdaughter?"

"They've followed us from Plainfoot. Bandits stick to an area and pick off travelers as they go through it. They wouldn't come all this way down the Long Path for just the two of us. We don't even have a pack animal."

Shory crooked his mouth into a grin. "You're sharp enough, Lordsdaughter. Sharp enough to give them sorcerer-scholars a run for their caps. I was to give you this before I left you at Tilde, but now seems the better time. You still have your private key?"

Tagg fished a long steel chain out from around her neck. The little key that dangled at the end was spidery and delicate with grooved teeth. Her father had given it to her before she left Morthigern. She warmed it in her hands as Shory pulled a small, flat box out of his satchel. The engraving on the box matched the key, its fretwork webbing out from a small keyhole. Tagg recognized it immediately as a courier box used by sorcerers for particularly delicate communication. Opening the case as-is would produce a garbled mess, but with the right key in the lock, the words would be clear.

Shory passed her the box, then turned away to give her privacy. Tagg inserted the key and opened the case, breathing in a deep scent that reminded her of her father's work room. There was a small cone inside the box, attached with a length of string. Tagg put it to her ear immediately.

"Taggerion of Morthigern, to the Lordsdaughter Tagglinde of Morthigern. Dated Seventeen Spring of the

Year of the Limping Fox," said her father's voice from inside the cone. "Tagglinde. Forgive me for not telling you this before your departure, but it was vital that you have no knowledge of these things should something befall you on the road.

"I will be brief. By the time you hear this, I will have declared war on our so-called queen, Floria, for the rulership of Sharell. It is my hope that the war will be over quickly, and my claim as cousin of our late King Din will be supported over that of his commoner widow queen. Even such, it is possible that Floria will seek to strike at me through you. Tagglinde, you must be careful, even at Tilde. Chose your company wisely and be aware at all times.

"I say this only as a caution, for Tilde has never become involved with any faction of the Sharellingyle wars, and is unlikely to do so now. You should be more safe there than among my chieftains in the Narnava. Learn your skills well and the next time we meet, may it be as king and kingsdaughter. Graces guard you, Tagglinde... and destroy this case."

Tagg blinked away tears as her father's voice faded. It had been three weeks since she had left her home at Morthigern, and the sound of his voice made her homesick all over again. Tagg set her mouth, wiping her eyes with the back of her hand. She put the cone into the case, removed her private key, then pitched the whole thing into the fire.

"My lord didn't mean you to worry, Lordsdaughter," said Shory. "Floria's not likely to try anything at Tilde."

Tagg fought to keep her voice from breaking as she tucked the key back into her blouse. "Those were her soldiers following us, weren't they?"

Shory drew his sword onto his lap. "And if one old Morthigern berserker can drop ten of 'em at a go, what are the odds of your father's scuffle lasting longer than this summer?"

Tagg smiled, pushing down her feelings of unease. "Of course, Shory. Papa is the greatest codecrafter in the world, after all."

"And you'll soon match him, Lordsdaughter," said Shory.

Tagg looked to the east where, far away, her father waged war on Floria. She breathed a prayer for his safety, then looked west to Tilde. Lights from the castle twinkled in the darkness. *When I am a sorcerer, I will be able to protect the people I love.*

[2]

They arrived at noon the next day, leading their horses over the causeway into the grand courtyard. Tagg supposed she should feel relief after the long weeks on the road, but the memory of her father's warning sent her to searching the shadows for threatening figures. Coupled with that, there was something about Tilde that just felt... off. There were no guards on the battlements, no flock of servants standing ready to take their horses, no laundry being done in the bubbling pool at the center of the yard.

Instead, a woman and a girl older than Tagg got up from where they had been waiting beside the pool and started towards them.

"We saw you coming on the outlook," said the woman. "Well met, Shory Bearkiller."

"Mistress Voss, by my word you are lovely still," said Shory.   He laughed and bowed.   "May I present the Lordsdaughter Tagglinde of Morthigern?"

Tagg curtseyed.   Then she caught her first full look of Mistress Voss.   The woman had three eyes!   And not in the spectacles-way, either; there was a third, brown eye planted squarely in her forehead that blinked and looked her up and down.   Tagg forced herself not to stare, imagining the swat her governess would have given her for being so rude.   "I-It is a pleasure to meet you, Mistress Voss," she said.

"You have Taggerion's look about you, for certain. Let's hope you have his brights, too," said Mistress Voss. "In any circumstance, I am the head of household at Tilde. Should you need anything non-sorcererly, you need only come to me."

"Of course, Mistress," said Tagg.   The woman had to know that eye was there, didn't she?   She had to, thought Tagg.   Perhaps it was some kind of deformity?

Voss looked back at Shory, releasing Tagg from her peculiar gaze.   "You may tell your master that Tagglinde will be well protected here."

"He'll be glad to hear it," said Shory.

"And on that note: Tagglinde, this is Melga

Hewenaven. She will be your mentor here at Tilde while you accustom yourself to our ways. Melga?"

The girl stepped forward. She was about four years older than Tagglinde, with curly red hair and a sour look on her face.

"It's a pleasure to meet you, Melga Hewenaven," said Tagg, inclining her head as she had been taught.

Melga jerked her head and muttered, "Pleasure."

"Melga, go get Tagglinde settled in while I have a word with Shory. She will be needing a frock and staff before tomorrow's lessons."

"Yes, Mistress," said Melga. "C'mon, Tagglindy."

Tagg hesitated. It was only when Shory motioned for her to go that she cautiously followed the older girl.

* * *

Tagg had to trot to keep up with Melga. The girl had a long stride and tended to flail her staff as she walked, and in the absence of conversation, Tagg took to studying her surroundings for enemies. Melga took a path uphill from the courtyard and turned south towards a well-kept area that Tagg would learn was called the Wizard's Plaza, distressingly full of nooks for a well-placed archer. Buildings of yellow brick lined the grassy lawn, which was crisscrossed with stone walkways and dotted with sycamore trees. Sorcerers dressed like Melga in burgundy coats with silver trim waved and called out to them as they passed, but Melga kept her head down and made for a small building nestled in the curve of the yellow sandstone wall. It was three stories tall, with narrow, slit-like windows. It looked sturdy. Tagg thought her father would approve.

"This is Meerwood. The girls live here, boys over in Greatwood," said Melga, gesturing to a much larger house across the way. She dug around in her pocket and tossed Tagg a key. "For your cell."

Tagg didn't have a chance to ask Melga what she meant by that before they were off again, into Meerwood and down a flight of steps into a cavernous basement. Melga rapped on a door with her staff and it opened, revealing a long, low room filled with boxes and racks of clothing. Tagg entered cautiously, keeping one hand on the wall.

"*light(4),*" said Melga, and four glowing orbs leapt from her staff to space themselves evenly across the ceiling. "Now you stand right there and keep still."

Tagg stepped into the chalked square that Melga had

indicated, her body tensing in case this was some kind of a trap. When nothing happened, she began to relax.

Then, the boxes and racks of clothing moved, jumping and hopping over each other as if dancing. Tagg nearly fell over.

"Yeah, it looks pretty," said Melga. "Then y'find it's just a buggy old bubblesort an' the magic goes right out of it."

Tagg had never seen sorcery at this scale before. She swallowed and composed her features, trying not to look like some backwoods bumpkin, but her mind was racing. She had seen her father's spells, of course, but always in little ways, like when he moved the dishes across the table or lit candles in his work room. He had kept the more powerful things from her, such as when he had to punish a subject or level a mountain. She wondered if her father's work was as complex and beautiful as this.

There was a purpose to the codecraft, for when the jumping dance had ceased, Melga grabbed the nearest items and tossed them to Tagg. "Should fit you," she grumbled. Soon Tagg was staggering under the weight of three long frock coats, sets of skirts, blouses, scarves, boots, and a bag edged with brass. Melga grunted, and the pile of clothes left

Tagg's arms to hover in midair.

They began the trek back upstairs, Tagg's mind humming. In all her worry over the bandits and Floria, she had forgotten how much she had *wanted* to be a sorcerer.

"Your room," said Melga, stopping outside a door on the second story.

Tagg dug out her key and unlatched the door. The room inside was small and sparsely furnished. A slit-window looked out over the sea, sending in a strong gust of the salty air that permeated Tilde. There was a bed, a desk, and a small fireplace; Tagg's haversack was already there, resting against the wall. It was hard to imagine that she would be living here for the next ten years. At least it looked secure.

Melga dumped the pile of clothes on the bed.

"Thank you," said Tagg.

Melga grunted. "C'mon, we still have to hit up the staffworks."

They left Meerwood Hall, and Tagg found herself walking in silence beside Melga. She should try to learn about the girl, if only to see if she was to be trusted.

"Hewenaven," said Tagg. "That's a Narnavan name, isn't it? You are one of my father's subjects?"

Melga shot her a dirty look. "I inn't anyone's subject—not your pappy's an' certainly not yours."

Tagg flushed. That hadn't come out right. "I meant to ask —you're Narnavan?"

Melga rounded on her. "And what if I am? I inn't about to bow to you, 'f that's what you're after. Let's get this straight: I'm a gold-chain sorcerer and you are a newb. I din't care what kind of treatment you think you're going to get here because you're a lordsdaughter. I came to Tilde to get away from you ladyships who talk pretty and think we folk have to stop our lives an' grovel whenever you take a whim to pay us notice."

Tagg felt her face getting redder by the moment as she fought to get her anger under control. She wouldn't let this, this *peasant* best her! "Then why are you my mentor, Melga Hewenaven? Mayhap there's someone else who'll be better at the job."

"I'm your mentor 'cause Voss said I *had* to, not 'cause you're anything I'd want hanging around me. She thinks you need your pretty little head watched all special-like, so *of course* I'm the one they make baby-sit you. Well I *inn't* going to watch some spoiled swot all day, so you just shut up and keep up. Then we'll work out how I can see as little of your face as possible."

Tagg clenched her hands into fists. *This* was to be her protection? Her father had killed people for lesser insults!

But before she could come up with a good retort Melga stopped in front of a wooden building with a large awning. The structure itself was simple and seemed more like a barn than anything else. Inside, Tagg could hear the sounds of hammers and files working away industriously. Outside, there was merely an old sorcerer smoking a pipe beside a rack of staffs. When Melga approached, he got to his feet and took her staff without a word.

"This is getting heavy, girl. What have you been running on here, haversack algorithms?"

Melga scowled and snatched her staff from him. "Wouldn't be an issue if you gave me an extra for the contests. And yes, I have been managing my memory." She jerked her head at Tagg. "The kidden needs her first staff."

"Bless me, another girl-child," said the sorcerer. "Partial to a particular core? I have some very nice Lindens, newly cut."

Tagg tried to smile at him. He, at least, was polite. "Thank you, sir. That sounds w–"

"She's a newb, she doesn't know what she wants," cut

in Melga. "Give her a Willows and make sure it's clean."

The sorcerer shook his head, then went to the rack of staffs by the door. "What's your name, girl-child?"

"Tagglinde," said Tagg, shooting Melga an irritated look. "Pleased to meet you."

"Polite, too," said the sorcerer over his shoulder. "You could learn, Melga."

Melga merely glowered at Tagg.

"Here you are," said the sorcerer. He offered her a short greenwood staff with whipping around both ends.

Tagg set the butt of the staff on the ground, and its top came up to her eyes. She had expected to feel a tingling, or at least something of the excitement that she remembered feeling when she had seen her father work his own magic. Instead, she felt... empty.

"That's sixty gigs of space for you," said the sorcerer. "Keep it in order and make sure you defragment it regularly."

"Defrag...?"

"Just keep your spells short and remember to get rid of what you're not using," said Melga.

Tagg barely had time to thank the staffworks sorcerer before Melga grabbed her elbow and dragged her away.

Once they were well away from the staffworks, she began to speak quickly. "Okay, kidden, listen up. Voss says you need special protection on account of you being oh-so noble, but I say I'm busy, too, and I don't have time to keep you from stubbin' your toe every second. I only gotta get you through your silver-chain, so here's how it'll be. I take lunch in the High Hall everyday at five o'clock. Third table from the door. You come find me, I confirm that you have not been eaten by wolves, and we go about our merry business. Elsewise, I have to come find you and be generally unpleasant about the whole thing. Voss may think you're the poly-bloody-time algo we've all be looking for, but you're just a newb to me. So don't forget it."

Melga stalked away, leaving Tagg enraged at the foot of the Wizard's Plaza. There was no getting past it. She would make Melga pay. No one said such things to a Morthigern and got away lightly, and they would certainly not start by saying such things to Tagglinde!

* * *

Shory met her on her way back to Meerwood. "A staff, Lordsdaughter? Your father will be proud."

Tagg was about to snap at him, but she forced herself to calm down. Shory wasn't Melga. He didn't deserve her anger. Not after he had protected her all the way from Morthigern. "Thank you, Shory," she said.

He smiled at her. A haversack was slung over his shoulder.

"You aren't leaving already, are you?" said Tagg.

"There's a ship departing for Vi Sharell in a few hours; the next will be in two weeks. By then the war might be over, Lordsdaughter!"

First the world gave her Melga, now it was taking away Shory? It was not fair at all! But she was a lordsdaughter, and lordsdaughters were strong. She forced a smile that she did not feel. "Of course, Shory. Give my greetings to my father when you meet him."

"I will, Lordsdaughter."

She held out her hand as she had been taught. Shory took her small hand in his big one and kissed it. The words burned in her throat as she thanked him for his company and his protection and bid him a safe journey. She told him the formal words, and that she was grateful for his kindness. She told him that she–

"Now, now, Lordsdaughter," said Shory, wiping away

the tears that ran down Tagg's cheeks.

"I'm sorry, I shouldn't," said Tagg. "It's just– It's just I'm going to miss you–"

"And what a comfort that is to this old warrior," said Shory. He swept her into a hug that she was sure her governess would *not* approve of, but she held on nonetheless. "Go ahead and let your tears out; you have a tough path ahead of you."

"I shouldn't– I'm my father's heir and–"

"And a twelve year-old girl-child who's never left her home before," said Shory gently. "You can be a sorcerer-Lordsdaughter tomorrow."

[3]

There was a list pinned to her door the following morning. Times, locations, and names, all unfamiliar to Tagg. She heard the bell booming the seventh hour and bolted down to breakfast, clutching the list then running back to retrieve her staff, which she had forgotten.

The High Hall was not so much magical as sparse. Few sorcerers were up at such an early hour. Those that were muddled through breakfast, trying to pour coffee over their porridge. Most were unshaven men, some of them boys just older than she. There were a few women absorbed in a pile of scrolls at the back tables. Tagg felt very alone.

After picking at her sausages and oatmeal, Tagg found her way to the hall called Anselm. It was one of the larger places, and fortunately for Tagg it was also well-marked and easy to find. As soon as Tagg entered she saw that the place resembled a storehouse more than a classroom. The walls were stone and shored up with plain buttresses of iron, the ground sandy, the roof merely loose thatch. There was a long table at one end of the hall covered with a pile of parchment and some charcoal sticks. Tagg thought it rather a large place for only a table, but her list said ANSELM 8 SGT. TUFTON and Tagg was not one to ask questions.

At the first toll of the eight o'clock bell, Tagg learned that she was indeed in the right place.

Sergeant Tufton was a middle-aged wizard with a clean-shaven face and a trim figure for a sorcerer. Tagg would learn that he had studied magic with a battlecaster when he had been a squire to the nobles at Hovigan, and kept himself fit for the day when he was called back to serve in his uncle's regiments.

In the open doorway behind him, Tagg saw six boys, three of them wearing the rank of silver-chains, and three of them brass-chained like her. The silver-chains nudged the younger boys through the door, but did not enter themselves. Tagg thought that these must be her fellow students' sponsors and felt a flash of anger at Melga. But before Tagg could dwell on it, Tufton motioned the brass-chains into the room and began to speak.

"So, you're this month's pack of popinjays?" said Tufton. "From now on you shall be Jay[0], Jay[1], Jay[2] and Jay[3]. Don't tell me your names, it doesn't matter to me."

"Why do I have to be 'Jay-zero?'" said Jay[0], a brass-chained boy with corn-colored hair and wide, sunburned ears.

"All things start with zero," said Sergeant Tufton. "You remember that and maybe you'll spend one less night with your lang-monster puking in your arms."

Tagg, who was now Jay[3], followed the sergeant and her fellow "jays" to the table. There were a few curious glances in her direction from Jay[2] and Jay[0], but Tagg studiously ignored them. A lady did not stare.

"Now, my little popinjays, you are here to learn the basics of writing, compiling, and casting your own spells. Any hooligan with a staff and a spell on it can cast a spell. It's the writing and compiling that are the tricks. By the time you leave my tender care, you'll know the mechanics of the process," said Sergeant Tufton. "I've got one more fellow for you to meet."

The sergeant went to a corner of the room where stood

a small paddock that Tagg had not noticed before. Unlocking the gate, Sergeant Tufton stepped inside and walked out leading the rope of –well, Tagg was not sure what it was.

Tagg had never seen an elephant before, but if she had she would have said that the creature looked something like a miniature one. It was about the size of a small pony, with brown, leathery skin and pointed ears. It had a long nose that snuffled a bit like a horse, and its feet were wide, splayed hooves. When Sergeant Tufton jerked the rope, it followed him sedately to where the students were waiting, chewing its cud the whole time.

"This is Ukan. He's a generation four Chree lang-monster, which is the language we'll be studying. He's old and steady but he's got a stomach like a lead bathtub and he'll take whatever code you feed him with only a mild fuss. Rule is, he messes on your code, you clean it up." Sergeant Tufton pointed to a broom and a bucket waiting ostensibly by the wall. "Now, which of you popinjays knows what you do with a lang-monster like Ukan?"

Jay[2], a tall, gangly boy with the complexion of a Bachiki, said, "We offer to Ukan our spell codes so that lang-monster Ukan may give us enchantments."

"Close, Jay[2], very close. The truth of the matter is that lang-monsters –any lang-monsters, whether they be Chree, Yava, Lithp, I don't care, all of them take the code that you write and turn it into magic spells. Once you write a code, you feed it to your lang-monster, and that lang-monster will return to you the power to do whatever it is that your code said. We as sorcerers can store that spell *on the staff*, as it is. You keep your spells there, and you can toss them off when they're of no use to you. That's writing, compiling with the lang-monsters, and casting," said Sergeant Tufton, ticking the three off on his fingers.

He had them begin by writing starter frames. The Jays sat at the table with books and sticks of charcoal while Sergeant Tufton wrote out the lines that would begin and end all of their spells. Whatever they chose to write would go between the brackets, he said, framed by the starter pieces. Tagg learned that no matter how impressive her codes were, Ukan would "encounter an error" extremely quickly if the code was not prefaced by commands to include and properly start her routines. Sergeant Tufton scratched a bit of nonsense onto a sheaf of paper and handed it to Ukan, then held out a bucket when the Chree lang-monster spat it back at him in a sticky green glob.

"That, my popinjays, is an error. See, Ukan's a nice lang-monster, he just spits it up and moves on," said Sergeant Tufton. "You feed a bad bit to Hessimells and they'll dog you for days to complain about it. No hard feelings, Ukan?"

Ukan blinked lazily at the sergeant, then went back to chewing his cud.

Then there were parameters. "Got to give something to get something," said Sergeant Tufton bluffly. "You call the function, give it its parameters, and it will return something. You want to add two numbers, you pass in the two numbers and it gives you the result. You want it to rain, you pass in *where* and *when* and *how much*, and you get a nice little thunderstorm."

The sergeant then set them to writing their own code frames. Tagg found herself copying out what Sergeant Tufton had written, but when he stopped to look over her work and noticed that it was not a precise transcript of his own writing, he had her do it over again. "Precision, Jay[3]," he said. "You tell the lang-monster exactly what they must do and they do it."

"Yes sir," said Tagg.

But Sergeant Tufton was not done with her. "Do you

want to know *why* you have to be exact?"

Tagg flushed. At Morthigern, she had never been allowed to question her governess. "W-why do you have to be exact?" she said.

Sergeant Tufton clapped her stoutly on the back. "It's because the lang-monsters can't *think*. They were bred to interpret exact commands. You can say whatever you want, but you must say it correctly. You might mean your spell to do one thing, but if what you write doesn't match your intention, your spell may do something entirely different. That is the beauty –and the downfall– of sorcery. We're not worth much without the lang-monsters turning our code into craft."

Tagg nodded, sinking down into her chair. It made sense to her, though she could not get over the feeling that everything was upside down. At home she always received a strict reprimand if she questioned her father or her governess. Is this how things were supposed to go at Tilde, she wondered?

At the end of the class, Sergeant Tufton reviewed their work and announced that Jay[2] would be allowed to give his code to Ukan. Setting the paper on which the code had been written before the lang-monster, Jay[2] stepped back and they all watched while Ukan snuffled at the parchment. A long pink tongue crept out of Ukan's mouth and licked the words from the page. Tagg, clutching her staff, thought that she could see the ghosts of the words sucked down into Ukan's long snout. She jumped when the lang-monster hiccuped, then Ukan's mouth opened wide and he blew a shiny silver bubble towards Jay[2]. Sergeant Tufton guided Jay[2]'s arm so that the bubble landed on the boy's staff.

"You've got the spell there, now cast it," said Sergeant Tufton. "Feel the weight of your spell in your mind and call it up, then project."

Jay[2] screwed up his face with concentration. For a while, nothing happened. Then, a burst of light. The words "Hello, world!" appeared in thin angular letters in the air before them, written in a golden-yellow light that flared once then faded away.

"And there's the beginning," said Sergeant Tufton. "I want you all to have this mastered in your practicum this evening, and I'll see you popinjays tomorrow for your next course of spellworks. Dismissed!"

As soon as they left Anselm Hall, Tagg found herself the center of attention.

"You're the newbie Lordsdaughter, aren't you?" said

Jay[0]. He turned to Jay[1]. "She is, inn't she? She's gotta be, don't you think? She don't look like a peasant, not by half."

"Oh, quiet yourself, Eddle," said the Bachiki boy, Jay[2]. "I don't see what all this fuss is about, she could be Floria herself and it wouldn't matter; we're here to enrich our minds with sorcery, not gape at the nobles."

Tagg squared her shoulders. Clearly, manners were not part of the curriculum at Tilde. She put on her best look of indifference and walked toward the Wizard's Plaza. The Jays followed her.

"Gape at the nobles? Why not gape at the nobles? They have all the real interestin' problems! My sister was a maid at the castle at Inns an' she said her mistress used to have herself painted with tomato paste an' rice flour so's her complexion'd get the hint an' turn rosy pale! What good is nobles if you can't gawk at'em?" said Jay[0] indignantly.

Jay[2] looked at Tagg suspiciously. "*Do* you paint yourself with tomato paste and rice flour?"

"No!" said Tagg. She stopped and faced them all. "Of course I don't!"

"See?" said Jay[2] to Jay[0].

"So, do we call you Jay[3] or do you have a proper

name?" asked Jay[1]. He was grinning, and Tagg had the distinct feeling that he was up to something.

"Tagglinde Morthigern, pleased to make your acquaintance," said Tagg stiffly.

Jay[0]'s eyes went moon-round. "Nah, not *Morthigern?* You're a lyin' loon!"

"I am not!" said Tagg. Her father had never allowed her to interact with young men who were not approved by both himself and Tagg's governess. He had said that it was for Tagg's own benefit. If all young men were like these three Jays, then Tagg fully endorsed his decision.

"You don't look like a Morthigern," said Jay[2], frowning.

"I am a Morthigern!" said Tagg. "How dare you suggest–"

"Whoa, whoa, Tagglinde, sweetheart," said Jay[1], holding up his hands. "What Eddle and Bashko mean is that, well, you don't look like a demon-spawn monster out to eat babies."

"*My muther says she knew a Ladysdaughter what had five babies–*"

"*Shut it, Eddle,*" said Jay[2].

"Morthigerns do not eat babies!" snapped Tagg,

looking at the three boys gathered around her.

"*She was a sorceress, too, an' she turned one of 'em inta a pony–*"

"Well, you can't blame *us*," said Jay[2]. "It was in the proclamation Floria sent last night."

"Proclamation?" said Tagg.

"*It was on account of havin' only four holdfasts to split between 'em an' she didn't wanna have to divvy them between five children–*"

Jay[1] was looking at her intently. "You must have heard, the riders came after practicum–"

"She is new to Tilde, she was not at the practicum," said Jay[2].

"*And a'course, they keep this pony in the stable an' whadyaknow, heir number two, he's going ridin' on his brother th' pony–*"

"What did Floria want?" asked Tagg, a cold knot growing in her stomach. She doubted that whatever Floria might say concerning her would be good. Still, she had to know. "What did they say?"

"Well, that Morthigern has invaded Plainfoot and means to enslave the Free Lands of Sharell with demon-magic sorcery," said Jay[2]. "That there's a bounty on the

Dread Lord's head, a bounty for treason, and a reward out for the capture of the Lordsdaughter —of, of you, Lordsdaughter Tagglinde. Of course, we codecrafters knew all about the invasion long ago on the leylines, but the demon-magic sorcery–"

"My father does not have demons," said Tagg. She turned on her heel and hurried away before the Jays could gather up to follow her.

You'll be safe at Tilde, her father had said. Suddenly, Tagg wondered if she would be safe enough. Could she be safe anywhere with a bounty on her head? And even if she was safe, would her father be?

"I have class," said Tagg. "I have to go."

"The beast up an' breaks his own brother's neck a-ridin' under a low branch–"

"Eddle," said Jay[2], "shut up."

* * *

In fact, Tagg did not have class at that moment, not for another two hours when she was scheduled for PRIVATE TUTORIAL RAIFFE 233 12 RUSHINGFOAM. Just moments ago she had been filled with wonder that her own codes might create the faint golden letters that Jay[2] had produced. Now she felt ashamed; here she was, doing *nothing* while her father was being branded a traitor to the land he loved and meant to rule by the rudest idiots she had ever met! Her father, the Dread Lord Morthigern, who was the *rightful* king of Sharell. Treason was an ugly word, one a lordsdaughter ought never use, but one that her father had used often enough in reference to Queen Floria herself. Tagg, for all she despised the queen and loved her father, could not help but wish that things could go back to how they were before the war.

She wished she could be with him. But that was no use. He was at war, and she could not help him there. For a moment she entertained a fantasy of herself, dressed in the black and indigo of Morthigern, side by side with her father as her spells... her spells... She sighed. What was she going to do, *print* stuff at her enemies? She was not a sorcerer yet, and even if she had been, her father had never let her participate in his plans before.

She found herself walking on a bridge over a small ornamental stream that ran in a circle in the courtyard before Anselm Hall. There was no profit in her worrying about it, she supposed. She stiffened her resolve. She *would* be a great sorcerer, just as great as her father. Then Floria would have two Morthigern codecrafters to deal with.

[4]

At noon, Tagg was lost. Raiffe Hall was nowhere to be found and Tagg was getting a knot in her stomach at the thought of making Professor Rushingfoam wait for her private tutorial. Punctuality, her governess said, was the mark of a true gentlewoman, and it would simply not do for her to be late. Of course, there were sorcerers walking all about, striding purposefully to one business or another, and Tagg tried to approach several to ask for directions. If only they did not move so quickly, before Tagg could introduce herself. Then there was the fact that many of them looked exceedingly unpleasant and reminded Tagg too forcefully of Melga for her to want anything to do with them.

I have a frock and a staff and I've already slept one night in that cell, but I still don't fit in, she thought. *Though maybe*, thought Tagg, watching a sorcerer walk by with a large grease stain down his front, *that isn't such a bad idea.*

She was walking along the Wizard's Plaza for the fifth time when there was a whirring behind her. She spun around, raising her staff –even if she had no spells it was still a good length of solid wood–

...and was confronted by a small, floating ball of water. It spoke, "There you are. Do follow, please. Lovely though the algorithm was to find you, I'd prefer not to spend time on searches just yet."

Stunned, Tagg could only nod. The water floated ahead of her, going behind the buildings on the north side of the Plaza to a little brick building shaded by pear trees and covered with ivy. When the floating water crossed the threshold, Tagg could see RAIFFE HALL inscribed on the lintel above the door.

Then there were stairs, and a corridor with moldy carpet. At the end of the hall a cherrywood door was open and inside was Rushingfoam.

He was a tall man in a small room –tall and skinny with a rumpled coat and a cap over lank brown hair. He smelled, and so did the room. Not exactly bad, it must be said, but of old vellum and charcoal and overripe fruit. It must also be said that the room did bear evidence of all three of these items. In addition to that there was a neat glass tank on the windowsill with a peculiar sort of fish floating in mid-air inside of it. It looked up at her when she entered, then went back to flicking through an immense notebook that had been set inside of the tank. Of all the things in the office, the aquarium looked the most well taken care of, Rushingfoam included.

"And here is Tagglinde," said Rushingfoam in the same voice that had issued from the water ball. "Do sit down."

Tagg gingerly moved a pile of scrolls from an ancient armchair and perched on the edge of the cushion. Rushingfoam rooted around in the mound of paper that was his desk. "You are my professor, I presume?" said Tagg, feeling that some conversation would be only polite. "I'm sorry I'm late. I couldn't find the hall."

"What? Oh, yes. Well, no. I'm not quite a professor. An assistant, if you will. But I will be, ah, professing to you in the matter of mathematical theory while I finish my thesis." He spared a fond glance for the fish in its tank, which paused in its reading and flew up to smack the top of the glass with its tail. "You may call me Rushingfoam. Oh,

I give up," he said, abandoning his search and flopping into a chair that was bowed like a hammock. "I had a list of questions written up, but I may as well try from memory. So, tell me, Tagglinde, what do you know about math?"

It was such a direct question that Tagg wasn't exactly sure how to answer. What *did* she know about math? Well, she had had a governess, her father had seen to that, and she had learned the harp and embroidery and reading and sums– "Sums, I can do sums," said Tagg. But there was more, though, wasn't there? "And my father showed me math with letters. I can do that, too."

"Oh, algebra," said Rushingfoam dismissively. "I will grant you that bean-counting has its uses, but it is rather... messy."

Tagg, sitting in a room that was more than likely crawling with mice and spiders, thought that was rather rich of him.

"To be a good sorcerer, a true codecrafter, one who writes and enriches the art, not just a simple spellwriter, you must learn to *think* like a sorcerer. If you write a spell to tell you the number of grains of wheat in a warehouse, how can you know that the count is correct if you have only tested it on a small handful? Most spells are called as a sort of series, that is, event number three must follow event number two and event number five must follow event number four where they build upon each other to a greater truth."

Rushingfoam looked extraordinarily pleased with himself, but Tagg's head was spinning. She didn't like to admit it, but she was completely lost. But she couldn't just, just *tell* Rushingfoam that! Years of manners and etiquette training told Tagg that her not understanding was firmly her own fault, and she swallowed nervously at the thought that she had ruined everything on her very first day of sorcerer training.

And yet, she would never improve if she continued in ignorance. Sergeant Tufton had taken it upon himself to ask her questions for her. Taking a deep breath and trying to suppress the feeling that she was doing something common, she raised her hand.

"So, given– yes, Tagglinde?"

"I–I don't understand these, these events, sir. Begging your pardon," she said.

"You don't?" said Rushingfoam. His face fell. "Oh... I suppose I should... oh, oh."

Tagg thought he was displeased with her, but when he slouched and sighed he looked more angry with himself.

"You must forgive me, Tagglinde, you see, I've never tutored before and I'm afraid that I'm not very good at this."

He looked so miserable that Tagg felt her own discomfort melt away. "I'm sure you're a very good tutor," she said. "I'm, I'm afraid I'm not a very good student."

Rushingfoam clasped his hands and took a deep breath. "Oh, dear, dear, dear, *no*. The responsibility is entirely mine. We shall just have to teach each other, I suppose. You must tell me if I am confusing or wrong or doing any other cloddish thing that impedes your learning."

Tagg nodded; she liked Rushingfoam already. Despite his appearance, he had the manners of a gentleman. "That sounds perfect," she said. "Did you, did you want to start again, then, with the events?"

"Oh, yes, of course," said Rushingfoam. "And I have had an idea. Come with me, we shall work outside. There is barely room to breathe in here, let alone learn."

Tagg followed Rushingfoam out of his office and they walked up a flight of stairs until he lead her out onto the roof of Raiffe Hall. It was a square, flat area with a wide parapet. A pear tree was growing along the right side of the building, and Rushingfoam went to it and sat in its shade, motioning Tagg to follow.

"Let's talk about cause and effect," said Rushingfoam.

"All right," said Tagg.

Rushingfoam pulled a case out of his pocket and set it on the ground between them. He opened it and motioned to the rows of tiles inside. "Do you know what these are?" he said.

"They're dominoes," said Tagg. A lump appeared in her throat as she remembered sitting up late playing games with her father. He had always let her win.

"Correct," said Rushingfoam. "And if you know these are dominoes, then surely at some point you have done this."

He swept a clear area on the ground between them and removed three dominoes from the case. Standing them upright, he placed them carefully so that the three pieces were less than an inch apart. They looked like a line of little soldiers.

"I am going to teach you about induction," said Rushingfoam. "Now, this may sound difficult, but it is actually quite simple. This is induction." He tapped the first domino lightly with his finger.

It toppled over, knocking into the second domino,

which in turn knocked down the third.

Tagg blinked, and waited for something magical to happen. When it didn't, she looked at Rushingfoam with confusion. "Induction is knocking things over?"

Rushingfoam smiled. "In a manner of speaking. It is a way of proving that something will happen in the future."

Tagg frowned. "What does that have to do with dominoes?"

Rushingfoam smiled. "Let's look at this a bit more slowly." He took away two of the dominoes so that there was only one. This, he stood up on its end. "Let us say that this is the zeroth domino."

"The 'zero-ith'?" said Tagg. "Isn't it the first domino?"

Rushingfoam laughed. "Sorcerers always start with zero. Later on, you'll see that it makes a lot more sense than you would think. After all, we all begin with nothing when we learn sorcery, is that not true?"

Tagg shrugged. If Sergeant Tufton and Rushingfoam were that keen on starting at zero when there was a perfectly good "one," she supposed she would have to go with it and chalk it up to a sorcerers' quirk.

"I now tap the zeroth domino, and..." he paused, doing just that. The domino hit the ground with a clink. "...it falls over."

He drew a piece of chalk out of his coat and wrote on the ground,

Domino(o) falls over when tapped

"Now, let's take domino one," said Rushingfoam. He picked up another domino and stood it up next to the "zeroth," so that both tiles were lined up. "Will you do the honors?"

Tagg tapped the zeroth domino, feeling rather silly. It knocked into the new piece and both fell down.

"So now we have Domino(1)," said Rushingfoam. "Which also falls over." He wrote as much on the ground beneath the line about Domino(o).

"You said you have learned something about algebra," said Rushingfoam. "So you are used to substituting letters for numbers. I want to talk about the *Nth* domino now. You might want to think of that for now as 'the next domino.'"

"So it's the third domino?" asked Tagg.

"No, it's the *Nth* domino. Where *N* could be any number greater than two, in this case. It could be three, it could be four, it could be seven million and twelve. Let's say that people in Sharell help us line up these dominoes for miles. We don't care which domino is hundreds of miles down the road at Vi Sharell, we just care that it is a domino in a line with all the others that have come before. Since we don't know the precise number that it is, we call it the *Nth* number."

"Isn't that kind of lazy?" said Tagg, before she could stop herself. She put a hand over her mouth quickly. She hadn't meant to be rude, even if Rushingfoam was going to be wasting her time talking about mile-long lines of dominoes.

But if she had been rude, Rushingfoam didn't seem to notice. "Not lazy. It's efficient. It's not the number of the domino that matters, you see, it's that the domino is representative of this whole sequence. Do you understand?"

Tagg pondered this. She nodded.

"Good, excellent," said Rushingfoam. He picked up the chalk and wrote:

Domino(N)

"Now, what do you think is going to happen to domino *N*?" asked Rushingfoam.

Tagg looked at the previous lines he had written. "I think it's going to fall down like the others," she said.

"Ah," said Rushingfoam. "This is what we call the hypothesis. That means 'guess,'" said Rushingfoam, noting Tagg's quizzical look. "Your hypothesis that the *Nth* domino will also fall to the ground. We are going to take this one step further, now. What do you think is going to happen to domino number *N+1*?"

"*N* plus one?" said Tagg.

"The domino that stands after the *Nth*. So if *N* is three, *N+1* is four. If *N* is one thousand and sixteen, *N+1* is one thousand and seventeen. Does that make sense?"

"I guess so," said Tagg. It made about as much sense as people not being able to label their numbers and calling them all *N*.

"So what will happen to the *N+1th* domino?" asked Rushingfoam.

"It will fall over," said Tagg wearily.

"But why?" said Rushingfoam.

"Because they all fell over," said Tagg.

"But why? We know that domino *N* has fallen over.

Why should domino *N+1* fall as well?"

"Because," she said slowly, "we know that the domino before it –domino *N*– is going to fall over. And when it falls over, it will hit domino *N+1*. Which will make it fall over."

"Precisely!" said Rushingfoam. "And, since *N* may equal any number, we conclude that all dominoes –*set up in a line like these are*– will topple over when the one behind it knocks into it. So if we tap the first one, it will set off a chain reaction to knock down all of the dominoes in the sequence. You have just written your first inductive proof." Then he wrote the last line on the ground so that it read:

Domino(0) falls over
Domino(1) falls over when Domino(0) knocks into it

Domino(N) falls over
Domino(N+1) falls over when Domino(N) knocks into it.

Since each domino falls when the domino behind it knocks into it, all of the dominoes will fall when the first one is tapped. Q.E.D.

"What's Q.E.D.?" asked Tagg.

"Oh, we all write that," said Rushingfoam. "It's something from an old language. Put it after your proofs. I like to think of it as meaning 'quite easily done.'" He smiled at Tagg. "And now you know induction."

"That's it?" said Tagg. "But– but that was so simple!"

"It is," said Rushingfoam. He looked slightly relieved.

But something was bothering Tagg. "Beg pardon, sir, but... but what does this have to do with sorcery?"

"Oh, everything, Tagglinde. Everything and more. Sorcery, you see, is not a bunch of set wisdom. We do not have thousands and thousands of separate commands at our disposal when we craft magics. We have only a few, which we can put together and build with." He leaned his back against the parapet.

"My people, from before I came to Tilde, built boats. And, I will tell you now, there are thousands of different tasks that must be done to get a boat seaworthy. But we didn't have thousands of different tools for each individual job. We had hammers and files and brushes and drills. And, using those in combination, we built boats. Codecrafting is much the same. You have loops and conditionals and switches, and if you order them properly you can do thousands of different things with the magic around you.

"So," said Rushingfoam, "if I tell you to write code to count the grains of wheat in a warehouse, you will perhaps write a routine to count the number of grains in a single cup. Then, how can you extend that code to take on the entire warehouse? You'll need to do that in some sort of sequence. And that sequence will often, in its purest form, come down to an equation very much like the one we just discussed. If you can prove that you can count the cupful correctly, the power of induction will show that you can count the whole warehouse correctly."

Tagg put her staff across her knees, looking at the chalked words thoughtfully. "I never thought of it like that," she said. "It makes sense, I guess."

Rushingfoam smiled exhaustedly. "I'm so relieved. I've been worrying about this lesson all week."

[5]

Tagg spent the next two hours doing what the Tildens called "earning their keep". There were a good many things that needed to be done around a castle like Tilde, and the non-sorcerers who lived there could not be expected to do all of them. So, the sorcerers took time off from their studies to help. Codecrafters of all makes and ranks cast spells to clean the rooms, wash the walls, tend the gardens and mind the bees. Silver-chains sorted books in the library or heated fires for the blacksmiths and the smithmages, who set aside time each week to mend any Tilden items that were in need of repair. The idea was to make amends to Tilde for putting up with the sorcerers. Tagg thought that it seemed fair enough. Her father had never approved of laziness, either.

Tagg, however, was only a brass-chain. Mistress Voss sent her to the langhouse to tend the lang-monsters.

The man in charge of the langhouse was named Bon Marett. He was not a wizard, but the wizards were all afraid of him. When he saw Tagg, he spat and cursed and Tagg thought she might have to hit him with her staff before he punted her to the compiler side of the langhouse and into the Yava pens.

Tagg quickly found out that not all lang-monsters were as kind and calm as Sergeant Tufton's Ukan. Yava lang-monsters, Tagg learned, were much like rabbits, at least in appearance. They had long, floppy ears and wet noses and were as heavy as a sack of potatoes. Tagg's job was to brush them and give them their pellets. This was not a difficult task except for the fact that the Yavalings, while toothless, had jaws as stiff as beartraps and would sooner gum her hand off than swallow a pellet, even if it was guaranteed to improve their optimization and give them glossy coats.

By the time Tagg left the stables it was five o'clock and she was starving. She had to report to Melga at the High Hall, but she could not go as she was. She would have to make a trip to Meerwood to get a new frock coat —one of the Yavalings had slobbered all over her.

There was a surprise waiting outside her door –a small ornamental box not unlike a courier case. It was intricately carved sandalwood, with three locks around the edge. But there was no key in sight. Tagg cleaned herself up and slipped the case into her pocket. As unusual as it was, she was too hungry to investigate. She would look it over while she ate.

Having lunch at five o'clock was out of the ordinary for Tagg, but not for the sorcerers, who were late risers by nature. There were more wizards eating now than there had been that morning, many of whom looked like they had just woken up. Tagg, feeling as if she hadn't eaten in decades, loaded up her plate with buttermilk biscuits and ham stew.

Balancing the plate in one hand and her staff in the other, Tagg sought out Melga. The sooner she got this over with, the better. Melga was at the back of the hall where she had said she would be, at a small rectangular table packed with gold- and iron-chain mages.

"M-Melga?" asked Tagg, approaching her sponsor.

"Scoot, newb, table's full," said a male wizard sitting across from Melga.

Tagg felt her cheeks going red, and her grip on her staff

tightened.

Melga turned around, then nodded when she saw Tagg. "See you found your way well enough," she said.

"Yes, Melga," said Tagg.

"Who is this, Mel?" asked the sorcerer who had told Tagg to leave.

Melga muttered something into her cup.

"What?"

"My sponsored," said Melga, gritting her teeth.

It was a mixed reaction at best. The sorcerer sitting next to Melga, a dark-complected girl with green eyes, said, "Why didn't you say? Move over, make room..." while a few of the others laughed. One said, "Melga, Melga, Melga, you do'nae learn, do you?" A tall, pale spellcoder on the other side shook his head, saying, "What did you do to Voss this time?"

Tagg, all too eager to get away from Melga, was suddenly hustled into a seat right next to her. She tucked in her elbows and began to eat steadily, averting her eyes from Melga's friends. Though her success in grasping Rushingfoam's lesson had soothed her slightly, she was still having a trying day.

The laughter began to die down, then the pale

spellcoder said, "Seriously, Melga, you must have done something bad to get Voss to shackle you right before the contests. What was it?"

Melga growled, hunching over her plate. "I... may or may not've been the one who left a duplication spell outside her door. At about... eye level."

The table howled with laughter. "*You?* You were the one who gave her the extra eye?"

"Melga, Melga, why?"

Melga looked distinctly uncomfortable, and shifted on her bench. "I...may or may not've been practicing without a sandbox in the Meerwood lounge..." Then she straightened and jerked her thumb at Tagg. "It ain't totally that, though. Voss says the little newb needs heavy protection an' a full-fledged battlecaster."

"Fine job you're doing protecting her, then, letting her wander about Tilde on her own," said the female sorcerer on Tagg's right. Tagg flushed. She could and she would take care of herself!

"Garn, I inn't gonna let her die," said Melga, glancing at Tagg grudgingly.

"Better not, or Voss'll really have your head on a pike," said the pale spellcoder.

Tagg busied herself with her meal while the older sorcerers went on to talk about other topics. The food was good, and she was hungry. Every so often she caught mentions of lang-monsters and induction. Melga was studiously ignoring her, and Tagg was happy to let her.

Tagg was picking at the last of her meal, the sorcerers around her chatting about something called a hash table, when Tagg realized that she still had the little box in her pocket. Drawing it out, she touched the locks, feeling a slight tingle and burn. She frowned. Here was, quite obviously, a magical box left on her very doorstep, and she didn't have a key to open it with. Holding the box in her lap as not to disturb her lunch companions, Tagg took the fork off of the table and slid it into the first lock, remembering once seeing her father do something very similar with the chains in their dungeon.

"What're you up to, newb?" said Melga, turning to eye Tagg.

"It was outside my room. I can't get it open," said Tagg.

With a grunt, Melga took the box from her and looked it over. "Present from one o' your noble admirers?"

"I don't have any admirers," said Tagg through gritted

teeth.

"Hmm," said Melga. "You want it open?"

"I suppose," said Tagg, affecting her best look of disinterest.

Melga lifted her staff from under the table and focused on the box. A couple of the older sorcerers looked at her with mild interest. "Well, it isn't encrypted. *Part(wood, pewter);*" she said.

The lock separated completely from the wood with a pop. Melga passed the box to Tagg, saying, "There 'tis."

"You are undoubtedly too kind, Melga," said Tagg. She turned her attention to the box. "What a strange thing, sending me a box I can't open," said Tagg, lifting the lid and reaching her hand inside.

"–I can't open," said Tagg, lifting the lid and reaching her hand inside.

"–I can't open," said Tagg, lifting the lid and reaching her hand inside.

"–I can't open," said Tagg, lifting the lid and reaching her hand inside.

"–I can't open," said Tagg, lifting the lid and reaching her hand inside.

"–I can't–"

Then she was coughing and gagging, sucking in deep breaths of air. Melga was on her feet, her staff smoking, the bench they had been sitting on knocked halfway across the room. The box was a pile of ashes on the table in front of her.

"Wh-what h-happened?" said Tagg, clutching her chest, "I–I kept going ar...around, I couldn't, I couldn't breathe..."

Melga was looking at her strangely. "That was an infinite loop, one o' the tightest I've seen in a long while..."

"Are you all right?" asked the other female sorcerer.

"O'course she inn't all right!" said Melga. She gripped Tagg by the shoulders, leaning down to look in her eyes. "Where did you get that? Answer me, that's a dangerous thing! You could've died, goin' round an' round wi'out gettin' any breath –where did it come from?"

"It was outside m-m-my door!" said Tagg. "In Meerwood! I, I just picked it up!"

"Who in the name o' my frightful zombie children wants you dead, girl?" asked Melga.

"I, I don't know," said Tagg. And in her mind, she thought, *who doesn't?*

Melga raked a hand back through her scraggly hair.

"Mayhap you really do need a battlecaster about."

Tagg was shaking all over. She could have *died*, just by opening a box. The confirmation that her life was truly in danger hit her like a knife, and her breath came in short, ragged gasps. "I need, I need..." She stumbled out of the dining hall, knocking over her plate as she went, not even bothering to apologize for the mess it made.

* * *

"Calm down, newb," said Melga, catching up to her at the Wizard's Plaza. "We gotta figure out who did this and then I'm gonna call them out at the contests."

Tagg sat down heavily beside the fountain and drew her knees up to her chin, shivering. "Why did it happen? He said I'd be safe... I don't understand..."

Melga, looking pained, sat down beside her and patted her gingerly on the back. "Highborn folk have highborn problems, my mam'd say." She growled, whacking her staff against a bush. "An' right before the contests, too! Blood an' bells!"

Tagg bit her lip, trying to steady her breathing. She wouldn't –she oughtn't cry, not in front of Melga, not even when her life was in danger. She hiccuped. "Wh-what are the contests?"

"Big tournament," said Melga. "Battlecastin' championship, as you do. It's in two days! I gotta place this year, 's my only chance of gettin' my iron-chain before this war o' your pappy's is done an' I'm out of use."

Tagg sniffed. "I'm sure y-you'll do fine."

Melga shook her head. She stood up, and began to pace in front of Tagg. Not looking at her, she said, "I can't watch you all the time, y'know. But...but when I go to practice, you come along so's I can keep an eye on you. Keep to the main paths, don't go off wanderin'. And don't touch, open, lick, move, or poke at anything if I ain't around. I'll put a protection on you, but unnerstan' that it ain't the best 'cause it's fitted for me, not you —you gotta ward yourself for the best kinda protectin'. You got that?"

"Yes, Melga," said Tagg.

"Good," said Melga. She glanced at the belltower high to the south. "I gotta go to lecture. You keep safe in the meantime?"

Tagg took a deep breath. "I'll try."

* * *

By the time she was at Spell Theory, Tagg had begun to convince herself that everything would be all right. Tilde did not take part in wars, everyone knew that. Too many sorcerers came from feuding families that the alternative would have been an empty school.

Perhaps it had even been some kind of mistake. Perhaps someone had dropped the box by her door by accident. There had been no key, after all, and Tagg would not have been able to open the box had Melga not broken the lock. Tagg tried to maintain this view as she sat listening to Professor Ailsonet talking about tiny magical particles that composed the world and could be harnessed by compiled source code. Yet for all that she thought she might come to enjoy Ailsonet's lectures, she couldn't forget the feeling of terror that had come from her time in the infinite loop.

She entered her late coding practicum feeling sleepy, worn, and somewhat guilty that Professor Ailsonet might suddenly pop out from behind a pillar and accuse her of not paying attention in his class (he didn't). Therefore, Tagg, keeping to the main walkways around the Plaza, entered Vyndium Hall with twenty other sorcerers. Among them were the Jays.

Other mages were already at work in the big

gymnasium where they were to practice their spellwork. Tagg was shepherded to a little space marked off with eight stones in an octagon. She had a desk and parchment and charcoal, as well as access to a Chree lang-monster stationed between her workspace and the other Jays'. Tagg saw a young sorcerer working with a Yavaling to juggle wine goblets in midair, and an older lady wizard using a thin, delicate lang-monster to divert a stream of water into three separate ones of ice, steam, and rain.

Faced with the blank paper to begin her Chree spells, Tagg forced herself to concentrate. She put the infinite loop out of her mind and focused on recalling exactly what Tufton had said about starting her code.

Okay, thought Tagg. *Let's try a main method. Like this...*

```
void main()
{
    printf("Hello, world!");
}
```

She looked at the paper for a long time. It seemed to be right. She coaxed the lang-monster over to her desk then set the paper down for him to look at. The Chreeling snuffled over the parchment just as Ukan had, then inhaled the words on the page.

Two seconds later the lang-monster had vomited a steaming mess at her feet. The harassed-looking man who supervised the session gave her a shovel and a bucket while glancing at her code. "He don't know how to *printf* if'n you don't tell him he needs that library."

Tagg winced. How could she have forgotten to include a reference to the code libraries that they had used that very day? Without knowing how to understand *printf*, the lang-monster would just, well, just do what she was now shoveling into the bucket. Jay[o], in the octagon catty-corner to her own place, was cleaning up a similar pile. Tagg glanced at him and looked away quickly –she did not want him spreading stories about *her* traits as a lordsdaughter. Jay[1], meanwhile, had gotten his code to compile and was printing a whole batch of rude words in the air before him. When he caught Tagg watching him, he printed "Hi, Tagglindy" and winked. Tagg ignored him.

On her next try, Tagg remembered the include statement, prefacing her code with *#include <stdio.h>*. This time, the Chree lang-monster did not complain. Tagg watched his stomach gurgle, hoping that all would work out, when the big animal blew a silvery bubble in her direction. Tagg held her staff at the ready, and hurriedly caught the compiled spell.

For the whole day, Tagg had carried around her staff, feeling that she may as well be holding any old stick of wood. It was useful for navigating some of the rockier patches of Tilde, but that had been it. The staff had been empty.

It was not empty now.

Tagg could feel the spell, feel it waiting like a little flag in the back of her mind whenever she touched the wood. "*main();*" she whispered.

The words, "Hello, world!" glowed in the air before her.

* * *

Tagg left the practicum tired but in high spirits. She had managed to change her code to print whatever she said when she cast the spell. It was a beautiful feeling to say something then see the words printed in the air before her, and she felt, for the first time, a bit like a real sorcerer.

Maybe Tilde won't be so bad after all, she thought. *I'm learning codes and math and, well, a bit of theory, I suppose.* She thought of the infinite loop. Buoyed by her good mood, she told herself that it must have been a mistake.

Just a misplaced spell, probably for that contest that Melga is so looking forward to, thought Tagg.

She reached her door and went to unlock it when a glint of metal caught her eye. There, on the floor, wedged between the carpet and her door, was a small, pewter key. The design and size matched that of the infinite loop box perfectly. Written in elaborate scrollwork on the handle were the words:

For the Lordsdaughter Tagglinde of Morthigern.
From A Friend

Tagg felt as if her insides had been frozen. She had been right before. No matter how much she wanted to, she could not deny it. Someone had meant for her to die.

[6]

Tagg spent the entire morning looking over her shoulder. Sergeant Tufton demonstrated the further use of parameters and set them to writing code, but Tagg's mind was elsewhere. When Sergeant Tufton asked her to compile her code for the class, Tagg was not even embarrassed when Ukan threw errors over her incorrect prototypes, only anxious that someone might sneak up on her while she was cleaning the mess.

After the spellcraft lesson, Tagg went to her room and locked the door. She tried to write up some of the homework Tufton had assigned, but her thoughts kept straying back to the infinite loop. More than anything she wished that her father could have been there. When Tagg's mother had died and her father learned that Lady

Morthigern had been poisoned, he had routed the whole castle of Morthigern before finding the man responsible, and when he had, he had turned the man's insides into his outsides. He would know what to do now.

But the Dread Lord was far away at Plainfoot, if the Jays' information could be trusted. Tagg would have to deal with her attacker on her own.

She put down her papers and buried her face in her hands. This was no good. She could not concentrate like this, not with all of the fear swirling in her head. If only her father was here. She pounded the desk with her fists.

When Tagg arrived at Raiffe Hall, she found Rushingfoam waiting for her outside. "Ah, Tagglinde. I heard about your, ah, mishap, yesterday."

Tagg's face fell. "I didn't think anyone would know about that, sir."

"Nonsense. One of our students has an allergy to the stew and runs out of the dining hall at lunch? Well, there's always cause for concern in the kitchens," said Rushingfoam.

Tagg looked at him blankly for a moment, then explained that it had been a mysterious box and the infinite loop that had nearly killed her, not the stew. Rushingfoam took this in with a look of surprise, then walked with her inside Raiffe Hall.

"That is a serious concern," he said. "Has anyone attempted to trace the key?"

Tagg shook her head.

"If your sponsor is indeed *the* Melga Hewenaven, she will be able to do it. Your attacker may be still here, and, if the sender is a Tilden, the matter will go before the Glass Council. Attacks by one sorcerer on an apprentice are not to be taken lightly."

Rushingfoam smiled at her nervously, clasping her on the shoulder. Still, Tagg could not quiet the fear in her heart. She remembered the feel of the infinite loop, the way her limbs had jerked over and over in the same motions, not getting any air, her vision clouding as her voice eked out the same words again and again, growing fainter and fainter as she used up all of the breath in her lungs. She wanted to run back to her cell and never come out. But she was a Morthigern, and Morthigerns did not show fear. She forced her voice to be steady. "Where are we going?" she asked as Rushingfoam passed his own office and started up the steps.

"The pigeon loft," said Rushingfoam. "I am going to teach you how to count, and we may need some pigeons to help."

Tagg thought that pigeons were not entirely appropriate given the situation. Still, she followed Rushingfoam up the stairs. At least Rushingfoam was a competent sorcerer; she would be safe in his presence.

Rushingfoam helped her into the huge attic of Raiffe hall. The room was large, spare, and covered in pigeon droppings. Feathers littered the floor and nests had been built in the cubbies of an old desk, in the scroll rack against the wall, and on top of an ancient mechanical loom. When Rushingfoam opened the glass windows, there was a rush of wings and an entire flock of pigeons flew into the room, landing on the carpet, the desk, the loom, even Rushingfoam and Tagg.

"Now, I know what you're going to say," said Rushingfoam. "You're going to say, 'why in the world do I need pigeons to teach me how to count, Rushingfoam? I know how to count.' Is that so?"

Tagg looked into his round, smiling face. "No, sir," she said quietly. "I was thinking that I don't know if I can concentrate on lessons right now with someone out to kill me."

Rushingfoam deflated, his shoulders slumping. "It

figures that someone would try to kill my pupil. I'm sorry, Tagglinde."

Tagg looked at her hands glumly. She shouldn't have said anything. It was bad manners, and poor scholarship, and hadn't her governess said that learning was a lady's most important leisure? Now she had saddened Rushingfoam, just because she couldn't deal with her fears the way a Morthigern should. She drew in a deep, shuddering breath. "I... I would still like to learn what you have to teach me. I will try to concentrate."

Rushingfoam nodded, shooing away a pigeon that had landed on his head. He gave her a sympathetic smile. "Let me know if you need to stop."

Tagg nodded, trying to clear her mind of everything but Rushingfoam's words.

"Let us say that you have six white stockings and six black stockings."

"All right," said Tagg, leaning on her staff. A few pigeons came to peck by her feet for crumbs.

"Well, suppose they are all jumbled in a drawer and you need a matching pair. How many do you need to draw out?"

"Two," said Tagg. "On account of having two feet."

"Ah, no, sorry" said Rushingfoam. "First, you need two of the same color. And you can't see which socks are which on account of it being dark. And you take N socks out of the drawer before turning the lights on. So, what is N when you'll be assured of having a matching pair, either black or white?"

"So I light a candle and see that the pair I get is a match," said Tagg.

"Tagglinde, you are missing the point of this question," said Rushingfoam. His voice was kind even as he chided her. "You are here to be a sorcerer. Learn, and gain strength. Then you'll be able to face any enemy who tries to hurt you. This may save your life someday."

"Sorry," she said. "I didn't mean to be impertinent." She forced herself to think about the question. "So I have twelve socks all together, six black and six white?"

"Yes," said Rushingfoam.

"Well, I need at least two, don't I? So it's got to be more than two. Hmm."

Rushingfoam steepled his fingers. "Think about this as separate cases. Here is your base case, your zeroth domino, so to speak. What could happen?"

"I could get a white or a black, I suppose," said Tagg.

"Then the next time I could get a white or a black, too. So, I could be lucky and get two whites or two blacks, but I could be unlucky and get a black and a white." *And with my luck at the moment, that would be exactly my case*, thought Tagg. *Except one of them would be spelled as an infinite loop.*

The answer hit her. "So I'd need to draw another stocking, oh!" said Tagg. "And that stocking would be black or white! And it would have to match with one of the other stocking, wouldn't it? So I'd need three stockings in total! It's three, isn't it?"

"Well reasoned," said Rushingfoam. "This problem is a good place to begin because it is an excellent example of the Pigeonhole Principle."

"So that's why we're up here," said Tagg, leaning on her staff.

"Yes. Let me demonstrate," said Rushingfoam. He leveled his staff at the flock of pigeons and corralled a group of them. "Here we have...seven pigeons. And this desk has, oh, we're in luck, six slots for letters. Now, if I try to fit *this* pigeon," he bent down and retrieved a pigeon from his group, "into *this* hole," he placed the pigeon in the first mail cubby on the desk, "and *this* pigeon into *this* hole... help me, Tagglinde, please."

They scooped up four pigeons and placed them in the desk where they were content to roost for the time being. At last there was only one pigeon left on the ground. Tagg went to pick it up, then hesitated. "There's no more room for it," she said.

"No, there is," said Rushingfoam. "It just has to go into a hole with another pigeon." He retrieved the pigeon and placed it in a cubby with one of the smaller birds. According to the laws of pigeons, it promptly relieved itself. "Our law is then, when we have more pigeons than places to put them, there will be a place where more than one pigeon must go: a cubby with two pigeons."

"So, that's rather obvious," said Tagg. "What does this have to do with stockings?"

"Well, let us consider reshaping our stocking problem. We have, in essence, two cubbyholes –two colors. If we draw out three stockings –or pigeons– in the dark, we are guaranteed to have at least two stockings that go in one hole –two stockings that have the same color, and thus are just the pair we need. Do you understand?"

"Well, it's not quite the same as having the pigeons, though, is it?" said Tagg.

"If the Pigeonhole Principle applied only to pigeons we would be in a sad state indeed," said Rushingfoam. "You start out looking for parallels. You'll get better at it over time when you get a feel for what to look for."

"And what does this have to do with sorcery?" asked Tagg. "I–I'm sorry if I'm being impertinent again..."

"No, no," said Rushingfoam. "It is good to ask questions. These principles I am teaching you are so that you can learn how things work behind the spells, beneath the libraries and within the templates that we as sorcerers use to change the world. If you do not understand where you are coming from, you will not be able to truly understand the foundations that your spells are built upon."

He put his hands behind his head and watched the pigeons scuffling as they flew from their cubbyholes. "I think that'll be all for today. I will see you tomorrow –no, wait, I won't, it's the contests tomorrow. I will see you the day after tomorrow, then. And remember to have Melga look at that key of yours."

* * *

Tagg left the sanctuary of Raiffe Hall calmed.

Allowing her mind to focus wholeheartedly on pigeons and counting had drained away the worst of her panic and she felt grateful to Rushingfoam for forcing her through the lesson. If nothing else, it had showed that she could learn the skills needed to become a sorcerer. That she would not always be helpless against attackers.

She would not live in fear of another attack. She squared her shoulders and took a deep breath. Rushingfoam had said to look for parallels. They had tried to get her with a box, thinking she would naively open it, and she had. Well, she would not touch any trinket or such that may be trapped. She had learned the hard way for the zeroth case, she wouldn't be fooled again on the *Nth*. And maybe Melga would know about the key.

Tagg did not get a chance to speak with Melga privately until after lunch that day. She had dutifully sat with her sponsor and the older sorcerers, but they had only wanted to talk about the contests tomorrow, though they did glance at Tagg a lot. When the other sorcerers had gone, Melga told Tagg to gather her things and follow her.

"I found something," said Tagg, once they were out of the dining hall. She took the key out of her pocket and gave it to Melga, telling her about the circumstances that had led to her finding it. She had wrapped it in a handkerchief, on the off chance that the key was poisonous. "It matches the box. Do you think you can find out who sent it?"

Melga picked up the key and sniffed it. "It's sorcery all right." She set it on the ground then walked four paces backwards. "I'm goin' to stacktrace it, all right? You stay right there."

With a noise like a whip crack, Melga brought her staff down in a strike that rent the air and caused Tagg to jump back. Faint silver letters appeared in the air before Melga, very similar to the ones Tagg had printed with her own spells. Melga waved her staff and the words began to move, scrolling quickly as Melga read them. Tagg tried to read the words herself, but they were mostly numbers, and the letters she did see were none she recognized, only *jne*s and *addl*s. At last Melga lowered her staff, the silver letters vanishing.

"It activates the loop, but there're nothing there to show ownership. They masked their IP –their Indigenous Placeholder address. I know the styles of most o' the battlecasters in Tilde, at least them's are here right now, but this'n's spaghettied somethin' awful. Sorry, newb," said Melga.

Tagg tried not to let her disappointment show; she had

hoped that Melga would be able to give her some clue as to who was after her –and how to stop them, if it came to that.

Melga sighed. "You better come with me. I need to practice for tomorrow, but I want to keep an eye on you. This's serious spellwork, an' I ain't gonna see my sponsored get cut to bloody sausage ribbons while I'm about, even if it's you."

Tagg looked at Melga abruptly –sausage ribbons? She should think not! But the older girl was smiling grimly, and Tagg decided that this must be Melga's way of making a joke. Tagg smiled back hesitantly. Bloody sausage ribbons indeed.

* * *

It turned out that Melga had a whole suite to herself in Anwe Hall. Tagg walked with Melga up to the eighth floor, her sponsor muttering grimly under her breath.

"You go an' get the sandbox, it's on the rack by my artwork," said Melga.

Melga's "artwork" was a series of stylish drawings of Melga doing what Tagg could only assume was battlecasting. Most of them were tournament listings, with

Melga's name fairly high on the billing. The box that Melga had sent her to fetch was old and worn, made of wicker that was splintering on the edges. Tagg picked it up and jumped when the box shook.

"Ha, it's just the partishes, Tagglindy," said Melga. "Bring'em here."

Melga set the box on the floor and opened it with a kick. Eight doors woven into the wicker sprang open and Melga took out eight pieces of shiny wood. At first Tagg was confused, but then one of them twisted and Tagg realized that they were not wood, but some strange type of worm.

"What are they?" asked Tagg. Melga offered her the creature and it settled onto Tagg's hand. At once, Tagg felt a cool sharpness about herself.

"Careful," Melga said. "Short answer is they keep my magic from gettin' out an causin' trouble –keep it locked in, understand? It's an eight-bolt spell, use it all over the place 'round Tilde. Keep these'ns apart and they generate such an attraction that it'll null your spells with these little'ns suckin' the magic out of the air tryin' to get to each other. We call it a sandbox." Melga nudged one of the partishes with the butt of her staff and the worms quickly formed a circle on the ground, stretching their lengths to touch their neighbors head-to-tail. Tagg felt a weird sensation, as if a cold wave were passing through her, then the partishes broadened their circle to encompass her as well.

Melga gave her a bucket of rocks and had Tagg toss them at her. At first Tagg was concerned that she might hit Melga, but the older girl simply blasted the stones apart with varying degrees of force. Tagg learned to duck whenever one of Melga's spells missed, though, because whenever the cast hit the partishes' barrier it would bounce back in a random direction before fizzling out.

Then Melga had her leave the rocks and fetch an old plant in a pot by the door. Tagg watched as Melga put it through a number of "splays," as she called them. At first Tagg was amazed at the bends and twists in the plant's long leaves, but by the end of the workout she was beginning to feel apprehensive. Melga was working the plant into something that best resembled a hat stand made of ram's horns, her muttered spells seeming so complicated and powerful to Tagg. She wondered if she would ever be as good as Melga, and if she would even live to try.

"That's all for now, I suppose," said Melga as she lowered her staff. She bent down to open the gates of the wicker box. "Go on in, partishies."

Tagg looked at the worms as they shrunk and straightened before vanishing into their cages. Melga's spells had been repulsed by the partishes. An idea struck her. "Couldn't I, couldn't I keep these partishes with me to, to keep me safe? If they can keep your spells in, they must be very strong, Mi– Melga."

Melga looked up at her, wiping sweaty hair out of her face. "Nah, this kind o' partish only keep spellwork from gettin' out, not gettin' in. Besides, they'd lose their charge if'n you kept 'em active for so long. They need their time in the hutch, else they're no good to anyone."

Tagg looked away. "S-sorry."

"Nah," said Melga, and there was no rudeness in her voice. "Better you ask than don't."

7

Tagg awoke the next morning to a clarion of bells from the clock tower. She peered out from behind her door and found that the halls of Meerwood were already full of sorcerers rushing back and forth from the baths, combing their hair, and putting the final polish on boots and staffs. Tagg, used to leaving her dormitory with half of its residents still asleep, felt lost in the commotion.

"Excuse me," she said timidly to a tall steel-chain with her hair drawn back in many intricate braids. "What may I ask is happening?"

"Where have ye been, newb?" said the steel-chain. "The contests are an hour away."

Tagg thanked the sorcerer; she had known that the contests were today, but not that it would involve so many sorcerers. The way Melga had spoken, Tagg had pictured a small group of battlecasters, perhaps sitting an exam together in Anwe Hall.

Upon exiting Meerwood, Tagg nearly ran into Jay[o], Jay[1], and Jay[2]. When they saw her, they froze. "See, tol' you she lived here," said Jay[o]. "All the ladies live in Meerwood."

"Uh...good morning," said Tagg.

"We wanted you to, rather we had hoped, if you would want to, I mean," said Jay[2].

"We wanted the pleasure of your company at the tourney today," said Jay[1]. He bowed, taking her hand with the sort of elegance that Tagg had never seen outside of Morthigern.

"Uh, thank you," said Tagg. "I mean, yes."

Jay[2], his mouth drawn up sourly, led the way while Jay[o] nudged him and laughed. Tagg walked beside Jay[1]. She hadn't wanted to pay much attention to her fellow classmates, especially not after they had said those horrible things about her father on her first day. But recent events had shown her that she needed all the friends she could get, and she decided she may as well start with the Jays.

She looked them over. Jay[o] was coarse and almost

surely a peasant like Melga; Jay[2] had the look of a merchantson. But Jay[1] could be a lordson. He was about her height, with fine brown hair and light blue eyes. His hand, when he had touched hers, had been uncallused.

"I am sorry that I ask this so late," said Tagg as they passed behind the great library, "but what are your names – your real names, I mean to say."

"Heh, o'course," said Jay[0]. "Narv Eddle at y'service. This'n is–"

"Simyno Bashko," said Jay[2]. "You may call me Bashko if you like."

"And I," said Jay[1], "am the lord heir of Quindoline."

Jay[0], or Eddle, snickered at Tagg's wide-eyed expression: she had known it!

"Nah yer not," said Eddle.

Jay[1] shot him a smirk. "If that suit you not, I am the son of a landless knight from Inns, my father wears the golden plume at Vi Sharell where he jousts for fame and glory at the court of Queen Floria. My mother is the finest harpist in all of Sharell, the damsel of the white kerchief and niece of the Lady of Dovina. And I–"

"Try again, Saoric," said Jay[2] –no, Bashko, he had said.

Jay[1] grinned, then struck an elegant pose. "I am the child of the lady mariner who took a prince of Ayri as her husband. I lived by my wits aboard the *Blue Buttercup* and pillaged the Isles of Fou as soon as I was old enough to hold a cutlass. I fought the heathens on the savage coasts of–"

Eddle punched him in the shoulder. "Such a liar, Saoric–"

"On guard! I protest, I will strike you down!" said Jay[1].

Bashko sighed and pulled Tagg aside as the other Jays tussled. "His name is Landel Saoric, Lordsdaughter. He is some type of actor, from Plainfoot, I believe. Do not worry yourself over his untruths."

Tagg bit her lip to keep from laughing as Saoric danced around Eddle, leading him away from the group until, in a sudden motion, Saoric pushed Eddle into a stand of lilac bushes and, by the sound of it, down a very steep hill. Saoric returned to Tagg and Bashko, dusting his hands off theatrically. "That's enough of the blackguard impugning my honor, fair Lordsdaughter."

"'Fair Lordsdaughter?'" said Bashko.

But Tagg laughed, and took his hand when he offered it to her, and together they walked to the great dueling pit.

Bashko followed glumly behind them, Eddle keeping his own pace as he climbed back up the hill.

* * *

The Pit, as it was called, was a huge circular arena with row after row of steps descending into the earth, ringed with marble benches and already filling with burgundy-clad wizards. At the center of the arena a flat dirt patch was being carefully inspected by a sorcerer and a snuffling Chree lang-monster. Tagg went with Saoric to the first empty row nearest the stage. She had never seen this many codecrafters together at once, not even at the High Hall or the Wizard's Plaza.

There were non-sorcerers around as well. Tagg saw Mistress Voss descend to the levels nearest the stage on the arm of a tall, portly sorcerer. There were nobles dressed in black and gray velvets with silk scarves and gloves that made Tagg long to be back at Morthigern with her own familiar gowns. Beautiful birds of green and red perched on the ladies' shoulders, their shining plumage glistening in the morning sun. There were men in cambric tunics ornamented with patches of fine silver chainmail, and little children in stiff lace garments that caused them to scratch at their wrists. Tagg, in her ungainly wool frock, could only sigh wistfully.

And there were others, not sorcerers, not nobles, who stood out from the crowd. They wore brown leather in intricate pleats around their chest and shoulders, and their hair was short and roughly cut. The regiment walked by Tagg without a glance, and when they passed down to the stage, Tagg saw the green sun blazoned on the back of their cloaks. Soldiers of Floria.

Tagg wanted to bolt, but her legs would not move. Soldiers? At Tilde? But Tilde had no allegiance, or so everyone had told her. Had Tilde allied with Floria? Were there other soldiers about, waiting to capture her? Kill her? Did her father know? She felt sick.

For ten agonizing minutes Tagg sat on the aisle's end. Saoric said something about Sergeant Tufton, something that didn't matter when there were soldiers about. He took her hand in his own, but Tagg could not draw away, would not dare move when any such movement might bring the soldiers right to her. Saoric was saying something, something reassuring? It was too much, too much to bear, not after the infinite loop, not after all that had happened–

Movement at the stage. A sorcerer walked out and thumped his staff. Speaking. No, stopping. Outrage. People standing up, leaning forward. Necks craning, then silence.

The regiment leader, tall and thin, sauntered to the center of the dueling arena. His second, overly pale like Rushingfoam, came to stand beside him. Swords, had they swords? Tagg swallowed, her throat gravel.

"In the name of her majesty the Queen Floria Sharellingyle the First..."

Tagg's heart lurched. All of it was forgotten: the codes, the math, Melga and Rushingfoam, Saoric sitting beside her...

"...The queen decrees that the thirty battlecasters who prove their courage and skill in this contest, given on the date of..."

Thirty battlecasters. Half of the battlecasters at Tilde, so said Melga. Including Melga. They wanted Melga, her sponsor...

"...will take their place at the hand of the queen's army against the usurper lord, the traitor, Morthigern..."

Her father. Tagg could see him, as clear as if he were there with her, his long, handsome features, his dark hair streaked with white, his thin, strong fingers to smooth her hair and tell her that all would be well.

"...thus commands the queen."

She stood up, her vision clouding, but it didn't matter. She tripped over Bashko, hurried along the main aisle. She had to get out of the Pit, away from the soldiers. Before, she might have believed that they would not dare arrest her, capture her, take her. Not in Tilde, not surrounded by sorcerers. She did not believe that now.

"Tagglinde? Where are you going?" Saoric was saying.

But she was already gone.

* * *

She dared not go back to Meerwood. The infinite loop box had been left there for her, and who was to say that soldiers were not already waiting? She drew her scarf further over her head until it shadowed her face. She started towards Raiffe Hall, vaguely thinking of going to Rushingfoam and asking his advice. But when she saw the soldiers congregating at the Wizard's Plaza, lounging and whetting their knives by the fountain, her resolve failed her and she darted into a heavy stand of bushes. They were the same bushes Eddle had fallen into just that morning, just an hour ago. Had it been only an hour ago?

The branches snagged at her frock, but she followed the wall around the Plaza until she stood before the great gates. A carter was there, unloading barrels and arguing with the porter. Yet even here were the signs of soldiers: their horses had been picketed by the gate. Tagg frowned. There were so many of them.

It was the first time she had ever felt this scared. The thought crossed her mind: *What if Papa should lose?* Would she exist like this forever, hiding from Floria's soldiers as Morthigern was overrun and she, its heir, sought out and captured? Made an example of?

I won't let him lose, thought Tagg. The soldiers had come for battlecasters, meaning that they needed assistance against her father's sorcery. Well, she was a sorcerer, too. Sort of. Well, she *would* be. But she could help with this. Floria wanted magic. Well, magic wasn't magic until it was compiled by lang-monsters and if they thought they could get the magic so easily they had another thing coming. She would make sure they never got their hands on a spell.

* * *

It was lunchtime at the langhouse. Bon Marett was feeding mice to a very satisfied Piython, and he scowled when he saw her. "Yer late, the Basycs are pract'ly fallin' apart for want of patches. Git!"

Tagg hurried away before he could start up his curses, and saw that in their pen the little fuzzballs known as Basycs were indeed starting to lose their fuzz. They *mipp*ed forlornly as she began rewrapping their bindings and linkings, and squeaked when she tugged them too tight. Her mind was not on the task. She was thinking about how to keep the lang-monsters away from Floria.

It was then that a soldier appeared in the langhouse. Tagg's heart lurched. She quickly ducked into the pen with the Basycs. They hopped and jabbered and climbed into the pockets of her frock, searching for inputs.

"...it's by order of the queen," said the soldier.

It was the same man who had spoken to the crowd at the contests. Tagg's heart lurched. Had he followed her here?

But the soldier, the captain of the soldiers, was speaking to Bon Marett: "...sixty lang-monsters are needed, to accompany the chosen battlecasters."

"Yer goin' pay fer 'em, sonny?" Bon Marett spat.

"I don't think you understand," said the soldier in a tight voice. There was the sound of a sword being drawn halfway from a scabbard. "The queen commands."

Bon Marett unleashed a string of curses, but they were suddenly cut off by a sharp smack. Tagg did not need to look to know that there would be a welt where the flat of the blade had struck him.

"I will expect them at the gate before the evening. And they shall be nothing but the best. Some of us are sorcerers, too, and we will know."

Footsteps, and the captain was gone. It was only when Bon Marett had reverted to his usual stream of profanity that Tagg dared rise from the Basyc pen. Several of the little compilers squeaked and had to be carefully removed from her frock, where they had been attempting installation.

Bon Marett saw her. There was a look of pure fury on his face, now marred by an angry red mark where the soldier captain had struck him. "You!" he spat. He did not pretend that she had not heard. "Go sign 'em out in th' ledger, or I'll have *yer* hide!"

Tagg left the Basycs keening after her and hurried to the great leather-bound book that occupied its own place of honor at the center of the langhouse. She had only seen it used once in the past couple days, when a distraught gold-chain had come in with his Chree limping behind him, in need of a new lang-monster to use while his old one healed. The gold-chain had written something in the book and left with a new lang-monster following him docilely. She herself had never gone near it.

The soldiers wanted sixty of these lang-monsters to compile and ferment the spells to defeat her father. There must be a way to stop them using the book. But how? She could sign them out the little Basycs, which hadn't been hired out in the past ten years, and which the battlecasters could not use. But the soldiers would know immediately and bring back the compilers for exchange. No, that was not it. There had to be a way to keep the lang-monsters out of the soldiers' hands.

She ran her hand down the column of Chrees, Piythons, Yavalings, Hessimells, Ruubies... what to do? There were other columns, and one caught her eye. Permissions. The Basycs that were in the langhouse and unhired had their permissions set to "–". What did that mean? At the bottom of the page was Ukan, a "rwx" next to his name followed by the name of Sergeant Tufton. That must mean that the sergeant had "rwx" permissions on

Ukan. Since Tufton had allowed her and the jays to compile code on Ukan, then "rwx" had to imply some type of use. Therefore "–" had to mean "no permissions."

A small smile crossed Tagg's face.

* * *

The hardest part was sneaking the directory out of the langhouse. For what she had in mind, she couldn't leave the book around for someone to undo her work. Fortunately, Bon Marett had slipped off, presumably to tend to his face, and she was able to avoid the other attendants who might have asked questions about the huge book hidden in her skirts. She darted as fast as she could toward the west wall of Tilde, looking for a place of safety to do her work.

There was a garden behind the High Hall with numbers inscribed into the flagstone path that wound through it. The sorcerers called it the Numbered Garden, though the sign beside it proclaimed it the "Cows Camping." Whatever it had intended to be before, it was quite overgrown with thorns and brown sandstone rubble. Tagg slowed her pace and, when she was sure no one was watching, ducked behind two slabs of stone that formed a screen from the path.

She took out the directory and a stick of charcoal. She started at the beginning, following the line of the permissions column. Whether the lang-monster was assigned to a sorcerer, brass to glass, she smudged out all of the "rw" marks, the "x" marks, the "u" marks and even the pluses and minuses that occurred every now and then. She replaced them all with "–". As she did, the words glowed and flashed silver.

The sun was down when she had finished; it had taken the better part of the day to edit the entire book. Tagg walked about the garden for a bit until she found a stone flat on the ground that she could lift. She hid the book beneath it, then hurried back to her cell.

Her fingers cramped from writing, she barely had time to lock the door before collapsing into her bed.

8

Tagg slept soundly that night.

The first lang-monsters to notice that their permissions had vanished were the Hessimells. Always finicky and always particular, when they realized that they were under the command of no one, they left their perches in the langhouse, the aquariums in Raiffe Hall, even the special greenhouse sphere that the Dean had crafted in his apartments. They congregated in the rickety old belltower, where they proceeded to mob any sorcerer that passed beneath them like so many angry crows. Angry crows that had bits of partially compiled spells in their gullets. Which caused flames to exit their mouths at incredibly high speeds.

An iron-chain wizard just leaving the library was caught up in a flaming tornado and deposited in the fountain, while his boots landed atop the staffworks and set the thatch on fire.

By that time, a Chree had noticed, and then there was a herd of Chrees of all ages, shapes, sizes, and versions stampeding down the plaza, kicking up holes in the turf and, because one never can tell what a Chree will do when given free rein, re-mortaring the brickwork on a crumbling corner of Greatwood dormitory.

...Tagg rolled over in her sleep...

Soon the sorcerers were among them, trying to slip lead-lines over the lang-monsters or reign them in with spells. Yet the lang-monsters of Tilde were resistant to spells, and few sorcerers knew the tricks to getting past their boundaries. Even the battlecasters had difficulty, for it was considered dishonorable to enchant a foe's lang-monster during a duel.

Then the first cook found that the Yavalings, too, had not only escaped their pens, but eaten the entirety of the kitchen garden as well as several scarecrows. The entire household was roused, chasing Yavalings away from the granary, all the while avoiding the Hessimells, who were in the process of capturing a tanner and leaving him atop the High Hall, where he stayed for several days among the gargoyles before a wizard noticed and helped him down.

The soldiers were perhaps the last to notice that something was amiss. They noticed very quickly when a Piython and two Sierpents invaded the guest quarters and ate a number of their belts and bootbuckles, though.

A group of sorcerers carrying a net full of Yavalings tried to rouse Bon Marett from the loft in the langhouse. He cursed at them and went back to sleep until the old Fourtan awoke and kicked out the back wall of the langhouse, causing half of the loft to collapse and Bon Marett to tumble into the icy Snowbol pen.

Melga, still awake and celebrating her performance at the contests, managed to rope a Chree with a lasso of starlight. She made a full circuit of the Tilden battlements before getting the animal to stop, and even then, it was only so the Chree could investigate an old seagull nest in the chinks of the wall.

Rushingfoam woke to find that the Hessimell that was compiling his thesis had broken a hole in the window and stolen his biography of Turing.

...and Tagg slept on.

* * *

Someone was pounding on her door. Tagg woke up and panicked. Was it the soldiers? Had they found her? She knew she shouldn't have come back to her cell!

"Tagg, y'there?" It was Melga.

Tagg let out the breath she had been holding and unlocked the door.

"Ah, good, you're all right," said Melga. Then she looked rather embarrassed.

"What's wrong?" asked Tagg.

"Nothin'," said Melga defiantly. "I mean– yeah, there's a lot wrong, but it's not me that's–"

"Didn't you win contests?" asked Tagg.

"Oh. Well, yes. But that ain't it, you– you don't know about the lang-monsters?"

Tagg's stomach jumped, but she schooled her face to be blank. "What's wrong with the lang-monsters?" she asked hesitantly.

"Slept right through the mayhem, did you?" said Melga. "C'mon, we'll go to breakfast and I'll show you."

There were few lang-monsters to be seen outside, except for a flock of jeering Hessimells harassing a sorcerer near the fountain.

"What happened?" asked Tagg, taking in the torn-up

lawn, the burned patches of wood, thatch, and stone, and the excellent corner-work done on Greatwood.

"Some idiot lost the permissions directory an' the little devils aren't listenin' to any one," said Melga. "All I can say is, 'Yay for this bein' after the contests.'"

Tagg smiled to herself. It looked like the soldiers wouldn't be getting their lang-monsters after all.

"Then, aren't you going with the soldiers?" she asked.

Melga snorted. "They inn't going to take me anywhere. 'Specially since yer great old dad's got my brothers fightin' for his side."

"Oh," said Tagg, trying to hide her relief. The soldiers would not have Melga.

"They made a whole passel of threats," said Melga, leaning on her staff. She laughed. "Even without lang-monsters, I still got enough juice to take 'em all down."

Tagg suddenly wished she had stayed to see the contests. Perhaps Melga really could take on a whole battalion of Queen Floria's.

"Watch it!" said Melga suddenly. She hefted her staff like a sword and Tagg ducked just as Melga brought the wood around with a hefty *crack*. The Ruuby that had been zipping toward Tagg's head reeled and flew off in another direction.

"Little snots is disruptin' everything," muttered Melga.

"Melga... do you know if the soldiers have left?" asked Tagg.

Melga snorted. "Naw, they're still here. A few silvers've decided to ship out with 'em. Leavin' tomorrow, from what I know. Though mayhap they'll go tonight if Voss can't get that Piython out of their quarters."

"Won't they need lang-monsters, though? They can't take sorcerers without lang-monsters, right?" said Tagg.

Melga gave her a long look. Tagg swallowed and blushed. If Melga suspected that she, Tagg, was behind the lang-monster mayhem, then Melga didn't say. "They've gotten a few of the old hand-crank compilers out of storage. For all the things they'll be able to code with them."

"That's... terrible," said Tagg.

"Very... terrible," said Melga. "Though I wouldn't like to be in the person's shoes what did this," she said. "Not when Voss and the Glassies get hold of 'em."

Tagg kept her face carefully blank.

Melga then went on to tell about the Sierpent lang-monsters' invasion of the soldier barracks the night before. Tagg tried to keep her laughter from being too gleeful, but eventually Melga had her laughing uproariously. What could Tagg do? Maniacal laughter was a family trait of the Morthigerns.

* * *

Due to the events of the night before, Tagg's codecrafting lessons had been canceled for the day. She did not see Sergeant Tufton, nor the Jays, though she did have class with Rushingfoam at noon. With the soldiers preoccupied in moving the belongings of their new silver-chain sorcerers, they were not out in force to intercept Tagg as they had been the day before. Nevertheless, Tagg was careful to keep her eyes down and blend in as much as she could.

Rushingfoam was in his office, staring at a huge book. Tagg started, thinking that he had found the directory she had hidden. But it was merely one of the big workbooks that the senior codecrafters used for their spells. It occurred to Tagg that she didn't know what level sorcerer Rushingfoam was. Probably a high one, as he had filled the entire folio with his small, precise handwriting.

Rushingfoam sighed, and threw the book across the

room.

"Sir? What is it?" said Tagg, alarmed.

"My lang-monster has run away," said Rushingfoam. He gestured to the aquarium that had held his Hessimell lang-monster. It was empty, the glass cracked on one side. "I am to defend my thesis in a week, and without these results..."

Tagg twisted her hands. "Surely... they will let you have more time?"

"They will laugh in my face!" said Rushingfoam.

"Oh," said Tagg. "Is there anything I can do?"

"No," said Rushingfoam. "I am doomed, doomed, doomed..."

"I... I am sorry." Tagg felt horrible. She hadn't thought that loosing the lang-monsters would hurt Rushingfoam.

"It's not your fault," said Rushingfoam, trying to smile.

Tagg felt more horrible.

"I had thought we might talk about the halting problem today," said Rushingfoam. "It is perhaps appropriate now that we remember our limitations..."

"I'm sorry!" said Tagg. She could not bear it.

Rushingfoam was her friend, the first to treat her kindly at Tilde. Others had been polite, but Rushingfoam had responded to her questions, helped her learn things she had never dreamed about and made her feel at home... and he had shown her that she could understand, and be a sorcerer. "It's my fault," she said. "I... I messed up the lang-monsters."

Rushingfoam froze. He looked at her swiftly, and Tagg could not bear to meet his eyes.

"I'm sorry," she said quietly.

"I... why did you do that?" asked Rushingfoam. His voice was tight, and she could not tell if he was angry or crazy or panicky or all three at the same time. "No, no, I don't care why, *how* did you do that? What did you do with the lang-monster directory? That is what you did, isn't it?" His voice was rising, and he laughed in a very unpleasant way. "I can't believe, *my student*... where is the book? Tell me!"

Tagg was shaking, backing away from him. She cursed herself: she couldn't tell him where the directory was now, not while the soldiers were still here. And yet he was looking at her with a half-crazed expression, and then he gripped her shoulders: "Where is the book?" he repeated. "I might be able to fix this– but I need a lang-monster! Where is it, Tagglinde?"

She broke away from him and ran.

* * *

There was shouting behind her, but she kept going. But where to go? Not to Meerwood, not to the dining hall, *certainly* not to the Numbered Garden where she had hidden the directory. She dove behind the buildings, away from the plaza, taking the back ways as she had done yesterday.

But she could not get away. There was the sound of running feet behind her, and she did not know Tilde well enough to have a proper bolthole in mind. She thought of going to the other side of Tilde, where the non-wizards lived and worked, but she would stick out there, where to go, where to go! To the langhouse? Yet because of the lang-monsters, because of *her*, the langhouse would be full of sorcerers, and she couldn't be caught, couldn't give them the directory, couldn't let them fight her father, couldn't let them–

She turned a corner, and ran hard into the chest of a

man in brown and black.

"Where' you goin–"

"I am most sorry–"

"*Stop her! Stop her!*" It was Rushingfoam's voice.
"*Stop! Tagglinde! Stop! Come back!*"

Her scarf had fallen back from her hair. The soldier
looked at her sharply. "Tagglinde?"

Then he smiled.

[9]

Tagg was jostled awake. Her head ached and her arms and legs were bound tightly. She tried to open her eyes, but could only see the darkest of midnight blue. When she breathed in, fabric pressed up against her mouth and nose.

She struggled, trying to free herself from her bonds. New pains flared to life in her neck and ankles. She tried to remember what had happened.

Then she did.

Her thrashing became more violent. She tried to scream. How could she have let herself be captured? How *could* it happen? She began to breathe in short, ragged gasps.

She passed out.

* * *

When she came to, the jostling had stopped. She was on solid ground, and could feel every rock and twig beneath her. Then she was turning, turning, and coughing and gasping and then light, light that hurt her eyes and made her shrink back.

There were soldiers all around her, setting up camp. Tagg felt a tug beneath her and she was knocked over. It suddenly became clear: they had smuggled her out of Tilde wrapped in a roll of cloth. Her hands and feet were tied with rope, and it was only when rough hands pulled her into a sitting position that she could see the face of her captor.

It was the soldier captain from the langhouse, the same man who had issued Floria's decree before the contests. And at his throat... an iron chain of Tilden codecraft.

"Awake now?" he said. When she struggled back from him he held up his hands. "Now, now, we don't plan on hurting you, at least as long as you don't make trouble."

"Let me go," croaked Tagg. "Let me go!"

"I can't do that... Lordsdaughter. You are Tagglinde of Morthigern, are you not?"

"No," said Tagg. "I–I'm Alia Smithsdaughter."

"The sorcerers at Tilde tend to think that you aren't."

"They're lying," she said.

"They were quite angry to find out you had hindered the lang-monsters, you know," he said. "It seems to me you might not *want* to go back there."

A thread of guilt boiled up in the mixture of fear and panic within her. It... it couldn't be true, could it? She hadn't thought that... no, they wouldn't... he had to be lying to her...

The captain could see the conflict on her face. "You just think that over, then," he said. He picked up a case that caught in Tagg's memory at once. The same carvings, the same handles... it was just the same.

"You," she cried. "You sent me –sent me the infinite loop box. You tried to kill me!" She began to scream, yell, lashing and kicking with all of her might.

The soldier backhanded her across the mouth. Tagg tasted the coppery tang of blood on her tongue.

"Quiet!" said the captain. "Do not make this difficult, or I *will* kill you. Floria has set no rules on *your* condition for me to collect the reward. Be sure I interpret that as 'alive.'"

He opened the case and Tagg saw eight slots inside. The soldier drew a short reed from the first slot and stuck it into the ground at Tagg's feet. Tagg shivered at once.

"I trust you've seen a partish before. You may as well know that these will prevent anyone *outside* from tracing you, and prevent you from doing any spellwork *inside*."

Tagg instantly felt her shoulders droop, and her eyes were difficult to keep open.

"Ah, yes, the drugging effect is another benefit. Pleasant dreams, Lordsdaughter."

* * *

When Tagg woke up the next day she was too tired to move. Just as the partishes had formed a sandbox for Melga's spells by stretching and holding each other head-to-tail, these partishes had stretched into a hoop on the ground around her. The soldiers had removed the bindings from Tagg's wrists and ankles, setting them just out of her reach beside the empty case. With all of her limbs feeling like lead, Tagg couldn't help thinking that she might have preferred the ropes if it meant no partishes.

None of the soldiers looked at her as they broke camp.

The captain arrived just as they were smothering the campfire, picking up the piece of rope from where he had placed it beside the partishes' case.

"I hope you've rested well, Lordsdaughter," said the captain. "Hold out your hands."

Tagg wanted to refuse him, but the draining effects of the partishes meant that she couldn't have lifted her arms even had she wanted to.

The captain grabbed her hands then tied them roughly, doing the same with her feet. Then he said a word and the partishes inched from their circle into the ornate case.

They need to recharge, Tagg remembered. She wondered if she could use the fact to escape. Having the creatures at a distance lifted some of the tiredness, though her bones still ached.

But any chance of escape that day was rendered impossible. The soldiers bundled her back into the groundcloth that they had used to smuggle her out of Tilde, but this time they left space so that she could look out from the roll. When they piled her into a wagon, she was able to watch the clouds go by while she struggled.

Think, Tagg, she told herself. *Struggling isn't doing*

any use.

Yet would escape help her any more? Tagg thought of Rushingfoam and his anger at learning what she had done to the lang-monsters. Would they even want her back at Tilde? Had they in fact given her to Floria's soldiers? She couldn't remember anything beyond running into the soldier, the blow he had given her had knocked her out cold. It was very possible that the Tildens had let the soldiers take her. And why should they not? She had made a choice, and she had ultimately chosen her father and Morthigern over the sorcerers and Tilde. If the soldiers had broken Tilde's neutrality, then so had she. Did she even have a place back at Tilde?

She missed her father. He never would have let this happen to her. He had sent her to Tilde to be safe... and Floria had broken the rules. Yet in sabotaging the lang-monsters she had chosen to be a Morthigern above a Tilden; she had broken the rules, too.

A thousand curses on the rules! thought Tagg. She had to think, think logically. She was trapped. Bound with ropes and the cloth, wound so tight during the day, and at night penned by partishes. She wanted a sword, a knife, her staff. Anything that would help her fight against her captors. But what good would fighting be? Tagg had counted at least thirty men in the company, and the idea that she could fight off all of them was laughable. Her better option would be to run.

She would have to run before they set up the ring of partishes. She had to force herself to move in the face of the coldness and lethargy that they created. She would do it tonight. Break free, then run west to the sorcerers of Tilde. If they would have her.

* * *

Tagg got three steps away from the captain and his partishes before tripping over her own stiff and heavy limbs. Another soldier caught her easily and she was once again bound in the circle of partishes. Her mind went numb, and she fought to think, think like they had taught her at Tilde, to meet the problem...

She slept.

* * *

From her prison in the wagon, Tagg watched the

clouds as she lay on her back, wrapped in the groundcloth. She could tell that they had left the coastal plains around Tilde. Around her, she heard the jingle and clang of the soldiers' horses as they rode beside her wagon. Tagg could no longer smell the sea, and the air felt foreign to her. She was tied tightly in the cart once again, sick with anger and fear and guilt.

Think! she told herself. *Think! There must be a way out of here!*

If she could only get the ropes off... but the soldiers were on horseback, and she could not outrun them.

If she could only run away at night, when they stopped to rest... but the partishes were too strong, she had learned that yesterday.

If only someone would find her... but had not the captain said that the partishes prevented her from being located? The partishes were only in effect at night. Perhaps the captain only had one set of them. Could the sorcerers locate her during the day, when she traveled, trussed up in the cart? Once again, the horrible thought came to her. Why should the Tildens come at all? After all, she had ruined their lang-monsters. She was alone.

She felt tears sting her eyes, but this time they were of

anger and frustration. If only she could fight them... but that was laughable, was it not? They had taken her staff, yet even if she had it, what would she do? She knew only the barest of sorcery. She was no battlecaster like Melga.

Think!

I can't fight them. Not them all. Not like I am now. Not like I am when the partishes are around.

The feelings of uselessness sought to overwhelm her, but there was the anger again. She *wasn't* useless. She had turned all the lang-monsters of Tilde onto their masters, hadn't she? Could she do something similar here? But the soldiers had no lang-monsters, they hadn't been able to get them from Tilde. Perhaps the captain had his own private lang-monster somewhere, but could she even get to its directory? Not given how far she had gotten the day before. Curse those partishes!

The partishes... could she do something to them?

They had no directory to sabotage, as far as Tagg knew. Just their little case, that horrible little case with the carvings and pewter handles, a matching piece to the infinite loop box that had almost killed her. That infernal case, with its eight little slots for eight little worms...

Eight slots, and eight worms. N slots and N worms.

The partishes needed to recharge. But what if there weren't enough slots? If there were too many pigeons for the holes, what would happen? There would be more than one pigeon in a hole. *N-1* slots and *N* worms. Would the partishes still be able to work if it had only seven of their number? She thought of the exact codes that Sergeant Tufton had taught the Jays to write. Precision was key. And seven was not eight, and though she didn't know what might happen, it was as good a plan as any. But how to accomplish it? She settled back in the wagon.

Think...

* * *

They took her out of the wagon and tossed her to the ground, the soldiers starting to set up camp. She strove to lift her head, to get her bearings on where they had camped. The sun had gone down nearly an hour ago, but the land was still lit by its afterglow. They had chosen to make their camp within a small copse of trees. Tagg wished for luck.

The captain came with his case of partishes a few minutes later. He took her out of the tight cloth and cleared a space before releasing the partishes.

At once Tagg felt the cold close in around her. The little water and bread they had given her that morning felt so long ago. Her limbs were leaden.

"Not long now, Lordsdaughter," said the captain. "We will be in Vi Sharell within the week."

Tagg decided not to rise to his prodding. She slumped over. The captain laughed and walked away.

It was a monumental effort to raise her head and remember what she had to do. Yes, there it was. The captain had not bothered to take the partishes' case away with him, just kicking it well out of Tagg's reach. Around her, the soldiers were bedding down for the night. She had to stay awake. She took hold of the skin on the inside of her elbow and pinched herself as hard as she could. It hurt, but it kept her awake. She kept at it until the camp had settled down, the few sentries more interested in what was outside than a prisoner that barely moved at all.

First, she tried to move her fingers outside of the partish circle, groping for the case. The embers of the fire had burned low, and she could only see the soft sheen of its pewter latch. But when she came to the partishes, there was a sharp shock to her fingers and soon her whole hand was numb.

She needed the case! Gritting her teeth, she forced her mind to act. She needed the box. If only she had some rope or string. She stiffened. She had the private key her father had given her before leaving Morthigern. It was still around her neck on its chain. She pulled it off carefully and grabbed the key tightly, letting the chain dangle loose. One good toss and... yes, the chain was looped around the latch.

Slowly she pulled the chain toward herself, stopping only when a sentry briefly turned her way. Then –and this was the important part– the chain pulled the box into the circle of partishes and within her grasp.

Remembrance made her hesitate. What if it was a trap? What if the box was rigged with another infinite loop, or something even more deadly? She would have to chance it. She took a deep breath and exhaled as she opened the box.

Nothing happened.

Nothing happened at all, and Tagg breathed in. There, cut into the wood of the case, were the little slots for the partishes. She took dirt and spat in it, making mud, which she jammed into the last hole of the case, packing it deep and smooth so that the captain would find nothing amiss should he glance inside the case. She crammed a few sticks into the slot as well, breaking them so that they completely blocked the hole. Then she layered it with more mud and smoothed it.

When it was done, it looked merely like there were seven indentations instead of eight.

I hope it's good enough, thought Tagg.

She scooted the case out of the ring. Then, exhausted from the concentration, her elbow aching from the pinching, she dropped off to sleep.

* * *

The next morning, she woke more tired than ever. There were a few crusts of traveling bread in her circle, and she had to make an effort to pick them up, chew them, and swallow. She tried not to let the anxiety show on her face. What if it didn't work?

The captain arrived, kicked open the case, and said a word to the partishes. "Good morning, Lordsdaughter," he said, hauling her up by her shoulder. Tagg heard the squeaking and scurrying as the partishes hurried to the case.

"Good m-morning," said Tagg. Already with the partishes leaving she felt her head begin to clear. Her body ached, but that she could force her way through that. She needed her wits.

The squeaking persisted. One of the partishes could not find a home to anchor himself.

"Hold out your hands," said the captain, brandishing the rope that he used to tie her wrists.

The squeaking was becoming more frantic. Tagg let her body droop, and her eyes found the case of partishes. They were scrambling about, fighting over the slots, attacking each other and prying out ones that had already docked in order to steal its home. The captain tried to grab her hands, and Tagg thought: *now!*

She pushed into him suddenly. Off balance, he stumbled backward, his foot landing in the case.

Then the partishes were on him, searching for an anchor point to recharge. The captain screamed as they crawled over his body. Tagg did not stay to watch. She ran, ducking through the trees, dodging the soldiers running to their captain's aide.

Tired as she was, her heart was singing. She had done it! She had met the problem and overcome it. Even through her failures, and perhaps because of them, she felt the sweetness of victory flooding through her, giving her the strength to keep running, keep moving, keep going. It was like casting her first spell, writing her first code... she had created something, solved a problem on her own... and it had worked.

She saw the picket of horses up ahead. Her muscles were on fire but she could not stop running. The soldiers had stationed their animals here and were readying them for the day's travel. She hitched up her skirts, grabbing handfuls of her frock and running through the undergrowth. In the dim light she hoped her brass-clasp could pass for a gold-chain, and that she could pass as one of the sorcerers recruited from Tilde.

"Quick, the captain's been hurt!" she cried.

A few of the soldiers looked up with concern. None of them dashed off, conveniently leaving her with her choice of the horses.

She grabbed the reins of the nearest animal and swung herself into the saddle.

"Hey!" said the nearest soldier. "You can't–"

"He's hurt, he needs a healer!" she cried, kicking her heels into the animal.

As she spurred the horse into a gallop, she heard another soldier arrive. "The prisoner's escaped!" he cried.

Then Tagg was too far away to hear. She cocked herself over the horse's saddle, doing her best to maintain her balance as she rode hard for Tilde. Her legs screamed at the pace, her muscles on fire as she fought to keep her seat.

The next thing Tagg knew there were hoofbeats behind her. She urged her horse faster and faster, crouching over its neck. She was the better rider, but her tired body could not sustain this pace much longer.

The grassland broke away before her, and then she could see the ocean at her left, the shadows of the trees falling away behind her. In the distance was the cry of the seabirds, and ahead, a mere spec of light on the horizon, was Tilde.

The soldiers were drawing level with her. Tagg muttered, "faster, faster," under her breath. She risked a glance at the soldier on her right and let out a cry of dismay: he was almost upon her.

Then her mount jerked. The horse's front hoof was sunk deep into a rabbit hole. Tagg had no time to react as the horse twisted and pitched her to the ground.

Tagg kept on the horse, but just barely. She hit the ground on her right side, the horse's body smashing her leg as it pinned her to the earth. She heard the hoofbeats of the riders begin to slow. She looked up and into the face of a soldier.

Then an expression of surprise lit the man's face. A burst of sudden wind swept him backwards. His horse reared, bolting off to the left. Tagg looked around wildly, but could see nothing.

She fought to push the horse off of her leg. Nausea swept over her as she tried; her leg was broken. She could feel movement through the ground beneath her, the agonized cries of her horse as it wallowed in pain. Then another gust of wind knocked Tagg's head back into the dirt. She threw up her free arm to shield her face. Someone was approaching.

It was Melga. "Are you filthy garbage collectors going to stand up to *me*?" she screamed. "I'll take you all!"

A shield of fire, its warmth blistering her face, burst up around Tagg. A whine escaping her lips as she jolted her broken leg. Then she saw Melga.

She had come on a small mountain pony, her hair streaming behind her, the new iron clasp on her frock coat riding up around her neck. She strode forward, and with a sweep of her staff there was an array of varicolored lights around her. It was a battlecasting array, and it was beautiful. Melga flicked her staff and three soldiers were caught up in a cyclone that sent them careening into the dunes.

Tagg groaned as more soldiers arrived and Melga was surrounded by a semi-circle of riders. But Melga was not deterred. She used her staff to catch up one of the lights of the array and thump it to the earth. Tagg felt a ripple go through the ground. Suddenly, the long snake-grass of the dunes bristled and wound itself around the legs of the the soldiers' horses. The frightened animals panicked, bucking and biting to free themselves, and more than one rider was pitched and trampled.

Melga whooped, for the few able soldiers were turning to run. But then, haggard and bent, a new figure appeared. Tagg shivered. "Melga, look out!"

It was the captain. He looked terrible. A long burn covered the side of his face and his coat was smoking. The partishes had done their work, but even so he was dangerous. The captain dismounted just as Melga's grass hobbled his horse, and though he was worn and weary he leveled his staff at Melga.

"No! She is my prize!" he said.

Melga laughed. She made a gesture, and it seemed that the very light of the sun was gathering in her fist. "*Your* prize? She's *my* sponsored!"

Tagg saw Melga make a wrenching motion, then the light flared. A halo went out from Melga's fist, and Tagg shielded her eyes.

The sound of the captain's screams accompanied her into unconsciousness.

* * *

It was sundown when they reached Tilde. Tagg rode

behind Melga on the sturdy pony, holding her sponsor tightly as not to fall off. Melga had splinted Tagg's leg as best she could, but Tagg still felt nauseous. Every bump caused new pain to shoot through her leg. She drifted in and out of a haze of misery, troubled by questions of what would await her when they reached Tilde.

Tagg slept.

The gates were open and Melga urged the pony up the path. There was a tall man waiting in the courtyard. Melga dismounted and found that he had walked around the other side of her pony to hold the reins.

Melga raised her eyebrows. She opened her mouth to rebuke him, but he held up a gloved hand. The words died in her throat. He lifted an extremely pale Tagg carefully from the saddle.

"I will pick up matters here," said the man.

* * *

The covers were warm and she could feel velvet against her chin. She snuggled deep into blankets of fine cotton. A hand stroked her forehead.

She awoke to the murmur of voices, far away inside a

dream. She did not open her eyes.

"I know that look."

Tagg woke up with a gasp. She knew that voice. "Papa!" she cried.

And there, sitting on the edge of her bed, was her father.

Tagg tried to rise, but could not. Her body was still incredibly stiff, her right leg splinted and wrapped in plaster. Her injuries could not stop her tongue, though. "How did you– What happened? Was it just– Tilde, and the sorcerers–"

The Dread Lord smiled affectionately. "No, it was not a dream, little Tagg. You have been healing for quite some time," he said.

"Healing? Oh– the soldiers– the war– what happened?"

"Everything is going to be all right, Tagg," said her father. "It is all over. Though..." he glanced over his shoulder, "I have been asked to find where you hid the directory of lang-monsters as soon as you awake."

"It's underneath a rock in the Cows Camping," said Tagg, straining to look at who was behind her father.

It was Mistress Voss. She gave Tagg a tight smile and

turned away. "I will see it is attended to," she said. "Taggerion."

Lord Morthigern nodded to her respectfully.

"I can't believe you're here..." said Tagg. Then it occurred to her: why was he here? To take her home? The thought filled her with a mixture of joy and sadness. She had missed him.

"Hush now, Tagglinde," said her father, making to rise.

She would not hush. "What is over?" she asked. "What happened, Papa? Where are the soldiers, and why are you here? What happened with the war? Are you king now? What is going on?"

"Do not trouble yourself," said Lord Morthigern. "Just know that all is at right."

"No."

"I am sorry?" said Lord Morthigern.

"No, I want to know. I deserve to know." She dug her fingers into the bedsheets and pulled herself up so that she was sitting. "Tell me."

Lord Morthigern frowned. "I had hoped that your manners would not suffer so much from being without a governess."

Then the door slammed open. Tagg jumped, but it was only Melga.

"You're awake," said Melga. "'Bout time."

"Melga, you must tell me what has happened. Where are the soldiers and why is my father here?"

"Tagglinde," said Lord Morthigern warningly.

Melga took in the scene, Tagg, sitting in the bed in her nightgown, the Dread Lord Morthigern beside her with mild distaste on his features, the irritation buzzing in the air... Melga's face split into a big grin. "Just imagine what she'll be like when we've had her for *two* months... your lordship."

"I am thinking that there might not be a second month," said Lord Morthigern pointedly. "If this is how she treats her father."

Tagg's face fell. She swallowed, and then looked into her father's eyes. "No, your lordship," she said. "But it is how a sorcerer treats a person she wishes to learn from."

"Oh, Tagg," said Lord Morthigern. "What has become of my daughter?"

"She's learned," said Tagg.

* * *

"But what happened in the war? It seems incredible that you could come here at all," said Tagg.

"That is a story," said Lord Morthigern. He sighed, and settled into a big armchair beside the fire. "You know that we were fighting Floria long before you went away. She is stubborn, despite her lack of royal blood. She would not acknowledge my claim to the throne. But then something extraordinary happened.

"I was preparing for our sortie down the Boros River when a person entered my tent. Imagine my surprise to see that it was Floria herself, who had slipped past the guards and come to see me in person.

"I had not seen her since the old king's wedding. She is still very lovely, but not quite the girl I remembered her to be. Of course, she is not as lovely as your mother was, Tagglinde. That is without question. I reached for my spells, but before I could do anything she began to speak.

"She told me that she has been against the wars between the provinces as much as I have, and that it has distressed her greatly to fight me, knowing as little about the ways of war as she does. And she confessed many other things that are not for you to hear. Please Tagglinde," he held up his hand before she could speak. "Some things are best kept private. Know that we talked through the night until we reached an agreement. The war is over."

Tagg gasped. "But, how–"

Lord Morthigern smiled. "How would you like to have a stepmother, Tagglinde?"

"Papa," breathed Tagg. "You can't mean–"

"Yes, yes, I had not meant to tell you like this. I will marry Floria and become king. Do not be so shocked; we have stopped the bloodshed and will have peace."

Tagg was dumbstruck. "I can't believe you're getting *married* and you didn't tell me! But... what about the soldiers who captured me?"

"Suitably chastised and sent to work in the silver mines of Ciso," said Lord Morthigern.

Melga had been quiet throughout the whole tale, sprawled comfortably on a lounge by the window. Now she spoke. "Y'know, I doubt it was really those soldiers' fault, since Floria, 'scuse me, *Queen* Floria, gave them the order and they had no ways of knowing–"

"Yes, yes," said Lord Morthigern. "But the Dread Lord of the North cannot go around being gracious to those who mistreat his daughter, iron-chain."

Melga laughed darkly.

Tagg exhaled, trying to shed all of the anxiety and suffering she had born over the past weeks. The war was over. Her father was safe, the kingdom of Sharell would have a good ruler, and peace. "But I must know... how did you get here so quickly?" said Tagg. "Did you fly?"

The Lord Morthigern laughed. "Now you are being silly. It is not even a two-day trip from Vi Sharell to Tilde by boat. At least, not when you have access to the royal fleet's sailormages. And now, Tagg, I have some questions for you, since you are apparently well enough to demand them from me. Tell me how you escaped Floria's soldiers."

And so she spoke, softly at first, of the soldiers coming to Tilde and demanding battlecasters. Whenever Melga made to stop her, Lord Morthigern held up his hand and let Tagg continue. Tagg told of the lang-monsters, and what she had done to their directory, not daring to look at her father or Melga for fear of what they might think of her. She told of her confession to Rushingfoam, and how she had run from him when he had demanded she set things right. She told of running into the soldier, and of being captured. She told of the partishes. And then she told them about her second sabotage, and of escaping the captain.

When she was done, she could only look at her hands. It had been tiring to remember all that had happened in the last week, all that had befallen her, all the rules she had broken. All of the trouble she would surely be in.

"Oh, Tagglinde," said her father at last. "Perhaps sending you here was not such a good idea after all."

"I have created quite a bit of a mess," said Tagg meekly.

"I'll say," said Melga.

"Come then," said Lord Morthigern. "I will have a man sent to pack your things. You shall likely enjoy court life, though I will have to see to finding you a new governess at Vi Sharell. You will want to say farewell to your instructors before we leave?"

Tagg nodded slowly, wringing her hands in the sheets. All of it had been for nothing after all.

Then Melga said, "Vi Sharell? You're taking her to Vi Sharell... lordship? Who'll teach her sorcery at Vi Sharell?"

"I expect Tagglinde has had enough sorcery," said Lord Morthigern.

"Had enough?" said Tagg, raising her head. Her father had a point. It would be easier to give up. To not have to deal with the Jays' pestering, to not have to bend her mind around Rushingfoam's difficult lessons. To give up the thrill and relish of creating, of changing the world around her by using her codes, her skills, her strengths... she could give that all up. But was an easier life really what she wanted? She made her decision.

"But Papa, I don't want to leave! I want to learn more, and be a sorcerer... Are you sure I can't stay here? ...If they'll still have me, of course."

"Still have you?" snorted Melga. "You think they'll throw you out for hacking the codes? If they threw out everyone who'd ever screwed up the system for one reason or another, I reckon there'd be only two people still livin' here!"

"You really mean that?" said Tagg, looking at Melga. "I'm not, I'm not expelled?"

"'Course not," said Melga. "An' besides, because of what you did to the lang-monsters they've decided to protect the permissions directory, something they'd never thought up before you came along. They learn, you learn, an' we all go 'experience plus plus.' This ain't the place to hold back, newb– Tagg."

"Did you hear that, Papa? I can stay! ...I *can* stay, right, Papa?" said Tagg, risking a glance at her father.

Lord Morthigern sighed. "Things will not get easier,

Tagglinde. Sorcery is a skill that requires diligence and patience. It is not something to master, but to meet as a challenge every day and keep learning. Your life will be hard if you stay, Tagglinde. But if you truly want to learn... I will give you my blessing."

Tagg reached out her arms to hug him. "Thank you, Papa." She looked up into his face, the stern, lined visage that she had known all of her life.

He was smiling. "You are welcome, Tagglinde."

* * *

She watched her father's ship leave the following afternoon. The south wall of Tilde overlooked the bay, and she stood there until the sails vanished into the east, leaning heavily on her staff to support her healing leg. She was sure he would make a great king. And she would be a great sorcerer.

Footsteps on the battlements caused her to turn, and she saw Rushingfoam had climbed up to join her.

"I'm sorry," she said before he could speak.

"You're– oh, the lang-monsters," he said. "I ought to apologize to you, it seems. I am sorry I scared you."

Tagg nodded. "I'm sorry I hurt your thesis. Did it turn out all right?"

Rushingfoam regarded her steadily. "The Dean was... more understanding than I thought. It seems his own dissertation took place during the Year of the Great Hurricane, and he said, at least when that happened the lang-monsters still worked. So he has given me an extension."

"I'm glad," said Tagg, shifting uneasily on her injured leg. "I didn't mean to hurt you, I hope you know."

"I know," said Rushingfoam. "But it is all in the past. Tagglinde, you have missed quite a number of your lessons."

Tagg blanched. "I'm sorry, I don't know if you heard–"

Rushingfoam raised an eyebrow. "Oh, and now it will be some story about how you were kidnapped and could not turn in your homework? You must think I am a complete newb to believe something like that."

Tagg bit her lip. "Well..."

Then Rushingfoam smiled. "Do not worry, Tagglinde. I am certainly not the one to begrudge you an extension. And if I was, your Melga was quite emphatic that I not penalize you in any way for missing lessons. She sought me out yesterday and, ah, gave me my orders. 'You be good to my sponsored or else,' were her exact words, I believe."

Tagg had a brief thought of Melga "interceding" with Rushingfoam. Probably threatening to turn him into a carrot, if she knew Melga. Tagg had not thought it possible that things could change so much between her and her sponsor, and yet they had. Many things had changed since her coming to Tilde.

And many things would change in the future. Her father would be a king –and she a kingsdaughter. But more importantly, she would be a sorcerer. And if Floria took it into her head to make trouble, well, Tagg would be ready.

"I am glad you are going to stay here," said Rushingfoam.

"Thank you, Rushingfoam," said Tagg. "I'm glad, too."

Author's Note

Tagg's world is fiction, but the words of her codecraft are not. They are drawn from real computer programming languages that people all over the world use to create everything from the navigation instruments in space shuttles to the graphics in popular video games. The language of the Chree compilers is based on the C and C++ programming languages, and can be learned by anyone with a computer and a little time to spend. Rushingfoam's lessons are both taken from real mathematical theorems, one of which really is called the Pigeonhole Principle.

About the Author

Erica Sandbothe learned her codecraft at Carnegie Mellon University, where she graduated with a B.S. in Computer Science and a minor in Creative Writing.
She lives in Pittsburgh.

Visit her online at http://www.ericasandbothe.com

Learn more about the world of Codecrafter at
http://www.codecrafter.org

Made in the USA
San Bernardino, CA
28 July 2015